Ohio State Parks

This Journal Belongs to:

....

....

Packing List

- ☐ CAMERA
- ☐ PARK MAP
- ☐ TRASH BAG
- ☐ WARM SWEATER
- ☐ BINOCULARS
- ☐ MAGNIFYING GLASS
- ☐ WATER BOTTLE
- ☐ SNACKS
- ☐ SWIMSUIT AND TOWEL
- ☐ FIRST AID KIT AND SNAKE BITE KIT
- ☐ HAT
- ☐ SUNBLOCK
- ☐ PEN AND PENCIL
- ☐ BACKPACK
- ☐ FIELD GUIDE
- ☐ DON'T FORGET TO PACK THIS BOOK!

Anything Else?

List of Ohio State Parks

PARK NAME	COUNTY OR COUNTIES	VISITED	DATE
A. W. Marion State Park	Pickaway		
Adams Lake State Park	Adams		
Alum Creek State Park	Delaware		
Barkcamp State Park	Belmont		
Beaver Creek State Park	Columbiana		
Blue Rock State Park	Muskingum		
Buck Creek State Park	Clark		
Buckeye Lake State Park	Fairfield, Perry		
Burr Oak State Park	Athens, Morgan		
Caesar Creek State Park	Warren, Clinton, Greene		
Catawba Island State Park	Ottawa		
Cowan Lake State Park	Clinton		
Deer Creek State Park	Fayette, Pickaway		
Delaware State Park	Delaware		
Dillon State Park	Muskingum		
East Fork State Park	Clermont		
East Harbor State Park	Ottawa		
Findley State Park	Lorain		
Forked Run State Park	Meigs		
Geneva State Park	Ashtabula		
Grand Lake St. Marys State Park	Auglaize		
Great Seal State Park	Ross		
Guilford Lake State Park	Columbiana		
Harrison Lake State Park	Fulton		
Headlands Beach State Park	Lake		
Hocking Hills State Park	Hocking		

PARK NAME	COUNTY OR COUNTIES	VISITED	DATE
Hueston Woods State Park	Butler, Preble		
Independence Dam State Park	Defiance		
Indian Lake State Park	Logan		
Jackson Lake State Park	Jackson		
Jefferson Lake State Park	Jefferson		
John Bryan State Park	Greene		
Kelleys Island State Park	Erie		
Kiser Lake State Park	Champaign		
Lake Alma State Park	Vinton		
Lake Hope State Park	Vinton		
Lake Logan State Park	Hocking		
Lake Loramie State Park	Auglaize		
Lake White State Park	Pike		
Little Miami State Park	Hamilton, Clermont, Warren, Greene		
Madison Lake State Park	Madison		
Malabar Farm State Park	Richland		
Mary Jane Thurston State Park	Henry		
Maumee Bay State Park	Lucas		
Mohican State Park	Ashland, Holmes		
Mosquito Lake State Park	Trumbull		
Mount Gilead State Park	Morrow		
Nelson Kennedy Ledges State Park	Portage		
Oak Point State Park	Ottawa		
Paint Creek State Park	Ross		
Pike Lake State Park	Ross		
Portage Lakes State Park	Summit		
Punderson State Park	Geauga		
Pymatuning State Park	Ashtabula		
Quail Hollow State Park	Stark		

PARK NAME	COUNTY OR COUNTIES	VISITED	DATE
Rocky Fork State Park	Highland		
Salt Fork State Park	Guernsey		
Scioto Trail State Park	Ross		
Shawnee State Park	Scioto		
South Bass Island State Park	Ottawa		
Spiegel Grove State Park	Sandusky		
Stonelick State Park	Clermont		
Strouds Run State Park	Athens		
Sycamore State Park	Montgomery		
Tar Hollow State Park	Hocking		
Tinker's Creek State Park	Geauga		
Van Buren State Park	Hancock		
West Branch State Park	Portage		
Wolf Run State Park	Noble		

A. W. MARION STATE PARK

Pickaway

DATE(S) VISITED:..

❑ SPRING ❑ SUMMER ❑ FALL ❑ WINTER

WEATHER	TEMP:
☀ ❑	🌤 ❑ ☁ ❑ 🌧 ❑ ⛈ ❑ 🌨 ❑

Address

7317 Warner-Huffer
Rd, Circleville, Ohio
43113

About this State Park

A. W. Marion State Park is a 310-acre (130 ha) public recreation area located four miles (6.4 km) northeast of Circleville, Ohio. The state park encircles 145-acre (59 ha) Hargus Lake and offers hiking, fishing, and boating
The 5-mile-long (8.0 km) Hargus Lake Trail encircles the lake. Mountain biking is allowed on a 7.3-mile-long (11.7 km) multi-use trail.
Wildlife indigenous to the area includes fox squirrel, ring-neck pheasant, a variety of songbird, a variety of waterfowl including mallard and the occasional loon, great blue heron, black racer snake, red fox, and white-tailed deer.
Boats with electric motors and rowing boats are allowed on the 145-acre (59 ha) lake. The lake is stocked with largemouth bass, muskellunge, bluegill and channel catfish.

CHECK IN:

CHECK OUT:

PARK HOURS:

DISTANCE:

FEE(S):...

WILL I RETURN? ❑ YES ❑ NO

LODGING:

SIGHTS

WHO I WENT WITH

ACTIVITIES

- ❑ ATV/OHV
- ❑ Berry Picking
- ❑ Biking
- ❑ Boating
- ❑ Canoeing
- ❑ Fishing
- ❑ Hiking
- ❑ Hunting

- ❑ Horseback Riding
- ❑ Kayaking
- ❑ Photography
- ❑ Skiing
- ❑ Skijoring
- ❑ Snowshoeing
- ❑ Snowmobiling
- ❑ Swimming

- ❑ Wildlife
- ❑ Bird Viewing
- ❑ ....
- ❑ ....
- ❑ ....
- ❑ ....
- ❑ ....
- ❑ ....

FACILITIES

- ❑ ADA
- ❑ Gift Shop
- ❑ Museum

- ❑ Visitor Center
- ❑ Picnic Sites
- ❑ Restrooms

- ❑ ....
- ❑ ....
- ❑ ....

- ❑ ....
- ❑ ....
- ❑ ....

Rating

⭐ ⭐ ⭐ ⭐ ⭐

Notes

....
....
....
....
....
....
....
....

PASSPORT STAMPS

ADAMS LAKE STATE PARK

Adams

DATE(S) VISITED:..

❏ SPRING ❏ SUMMER ❏ FALL ❏ WINTER

WEATHER			TEMP:		
☀	❄☁	☁	🌧	⛈	🌨
❏	❏	❏	❏	❏	❏

Address

14633 State Rte 41,
West Union, Ohio
45693

About this State Park

Adams Lake State Park is a public recreation area that surrounds Adams Lake on the far northern edge of the village of West Union, Adams County, The park's 96 acres (39 ha) are equally divided between land and water and include a rare dry-prairie remnant, Adams Lake Prairie State Nature Preserve. The park offers fishing, boating, picnicking, and hiking.

CHECK IN:

CHECK OUT:

PARK HOURS:

DISTANCE:

FEE(S):..

WILL I RETURN? ❏ YES ❏ NO

LODGING:

SIGHTS

WHO I WENT WITH

ACTIVITIES

- ❏ ATV/OHV
- ❏ Berry Picking
- ❏ Biking
- ❏ Boating
- ❏ Canoeing
- ❏ Fishing
- ❏ Hiking
- ❏ Hunting

- ❏ Horseback Riding
- ❏ Kayaking
- ❏ Photography
- ❏ Skiing
- ❏ Skijoring
- ❏ Snowshoeing
- ❏ Snowmobiling
- ❏ Swimming

- ❏ Wildlife
- ❏ Bird Viewing
- ❏ ....
- ❏ ....
- ❏ ....
- ❏ ....
- ❏ ....
- ❏ ....

FACILITIES

- ❏ ADA
- ❏ Gift Shop
- ❏ Museum

- ❏ Visitor Center
- ❏ Picnic Sites
- ❏ Restrooms

- ❏ ....
- ❏ ....
- ❏ ....

- ❏ ....
- ❏ ....
- ❏ ....

Rating

★ ★ ★ ★ ★

Notes

....
....
....
....
....
....
....
....

PASSPORT STAMPS

ALUM CREEK STATE PARK

Delaware

DATE(S) VISITED:..

❑ SPRING ❑ SUMMER ❑ FALL ❑ WINTER

WEATHER			TEMP:		
❑	❑	❑	❑	❑	❑

Address

3305 S Old State Rd
Delaware, Ohio 43015

About this State Park

Alum Creek's large reservoir and gently rolling span of fields and woodlands provides a hub of recreational activity just minutes from Ohio's capital city. Quiet coves nestled among shale cliffs await the solitary fisherman in the park's northern reaches while sunseekers mingle with thousands on Ohio's largest inland beach.
Alum Creek's 297 family campsites offer both wooded and sunny areas, some of which overlook the lake. This well-designed campground has a beach and a boat ramp for exclusive use of the overnight guests. Each site has an electrical hookup, and heated shower facilities are located throughout the facility.

CHECK IN:

CHECK OUT:

PARK HOURS:

DISTANCE:

FEE(S):..

WILL I RETURN?   ❑ YES   ❑ NO

LODGING:

SIGHTS

WHO I WENT WITH

ACTIVITIES

- ❑ ATV/OHV
- ❑ Berry Picking
- ❑ Biking
- ❑ Boating
- ❑ Canoeing
- ❑ Fishing
- ❑ Hiking
- ❑ Hunting

- ❑ Horseback Riding
- ❑ Kayaking
- ❑ Photography
- ❑ Skiing
- ❑ Skijoring
- ❑ Snowshoeing
- ❑ Snowmobiling
- ❑ Swimming

- ❑ Wildlife
- ❑ Bird Viewing
- ❑ ....
- ❑ ....
- ❑ ....
- ❑ ....
- ❑ ....
- ❑ ....

FACILITIES

- ❑ ADA
- ❑ Gift Shop
- ❑ Museum

- ❑ Visitor Center
- ❑ Picnic Sites
- ❑ Restrooms

- ❑ ....
- ❑ ....
- ❑ ....

- ❑ ....
- ❑ ....
- ❑ ....

Rating

⭐ ⭐ ⭐ ⭐ ⭐

Notes

....
....
....
....
....
....
....
....

PASSPORT STAMPS

BARKCAMP STATE PARK

Belmont

DATE(S) VISITED:..

❑ SPRING   ❑ SUMMER   ❑ FALL   ❑ WINTER

WEATHER	TEMP:

❑   ❑   ❑   ❑   ❑   ❑

Address

65330 Barkcamp Park
Rd, Belmont, Ohio
43718

About this State Park

Belmont County's rugged hills provide the backdrop for picturesque Barkcamp State Park. In addition to fine recreational facilities, visitors will enjoy the mature woodlands, open meadows, scenic lake and abundant wildlife of this secluded park.
Barkcamp offers 150 electrified campsites in sunny and shaded areas. The campground features hot showers, tables, firerings, two wheelchair accessible sites and a dump station. A group camp that accommodates 15 sites is available for organized groups by reservation. In addition, a horseman's camp with 25 sites is available. Five Rent-A-Camp units consisting of a tent, dining canopy, cooler, cookstove and other equipment can be rented during the summer months by reservation. Pet camping is permitted on designated sites.

CHECK IN:

CHECK OUT:

PARK HOURS:

DISTANCE:

FEE(S):..

WILL I RETURN?   ❑ YES   ❑ NO

LODGING:

SIGHTS

WHO I WENT WITH

ACTIVITIES

- ❏ ATV/OHV
- ❏ Berry Picking
- ❏ Biking
- ❏ Boating
- ❏ Canoeing
- ❏ Fishing
- ❏ Hiking
- ❏ Hunting

- ❏ Horseback Riding
- ❏ Kayaking
- ❏ Photography
- ❏ Skiing
- ❏ Skijoring
- ❏ Snowshoeing
- ❏ Snowmobiling
- ❏ Swimming

- ❏ Wildlife
- ❏ Bird Viewing
- ❏ ....
- ❏ ....
- ❏ ....
- ❏ ....
- ❏ ....
- ❏ ....

FACILITIES

- ❏ ADA
- ❏ Gift Shop
- ❏ Museum

- ❏ Visitor Center
- ❏ Picnic Sites
- ❏ Restrooms

- ❏ ....
- ❏ ....
- ❏ ....

- ❏ ....
- ❏ ....
- ❏ ....

Rating

⭐ ⭐ ⭐ ⭐ ⭐

Notes

....
....
....
....
....
....
....
....

PASSPORT STAMPS

BUCK CREEK STATE PARK

Clark

DATE(S) VISITED:...

❏ SPRING ❏ SUMMER ❏ FALL ❏ WINTER

WEATHER			TEMP:		
☀	☁	☁	☁	☁	☁
❏	❏	❏	❏	❏	❏

Address

976 Buck Creek Ln,
Springfield, Ohio
45502

About this State Park

Buck Creek State Park is a 4,016-acre (1,625 ha) public recreation area in Clark County, that is leased by the state of Ohio from the U.S. Army Corps of Engineers. The state park's main feature is the C. J. Brown Reservoir, a flood control reservoir created by the USACE on Buck Creek (or Lagonda Creek) as part of a flood control system in the Ohio River drainage basin.
The park offers swimming, fishing, camping, cabins, boating, 5.5 miles (8.9 km) of hiking trails, 7.5 miles (12.1 km) of bridle trails, winter recreation, and seasonal hunting. Common game fish include walleye, white bass, and crappie.

CHECK IN:

CHECK OUT:

PARK HOURS:

DISTANCE:

FEE(S):...

WILL I RETURN? ❏ YES ❏ NO

LODGING:

SIGHTS

WHO I WENT WITH

ACTIVITIES

❑ ATV/OHV	❑ Horseback Riding	❑ Wildlife
❑ Berry Picking	❑ Kayaking	❑ Bird Viewing
❑ Biking	❑ Photography	❑ ....
❑ Boating	❑ Skiing	❑ ....
❑ Canoeing	❑ Skijoring	❑ ....
❑ Fishing	❑ Snowshoeing	❑ ....
❑ Hiking	❑ Snowmobiling	❑ ....
❑ Hunting	❑ Swimming	❑ ....

FACILITIES

❑ ADA	❑ Visitor Center	❑	❑ ....
❑ Gift Shop	❑ Picnic Sites	❑	❑ ....
❑ Museum	❑ Restrooms	❑	❑ ....

Rating

★ ★ ★ ★ ★

Notes

....
....
....
....
....
....
....
....

PASSPORT STAMPS

CAESAR CREEK STATE PARK

Warren, Clinton, Greene

DATE(S) VISITED:...

❏ SPRING ❏ SUMMER ❏ FALL ❏ WINTER

WEATHER			TEMP:		
❏	❏	❏	❏	❏	❏

Address

8570 OH-73, Waynesville, Ohio 45068

About this State Park

Caesar Creek State Park is a public recreation area located in southwestern Ohio, five miles (8 km) east of Waynesville, in Warren, Clinton, and Greene counties. The park is leased by the State from the U.S. Army Corps of Engineers, who in the 1970s erected a dam on Caesar Creek to impound a 2,830-acre (1,150 ha) lake. The total park area, including the lake, is 7,530-acre (3,050 ha).
Caesar Creek State Park is highlighted by clear blue waters, scattered woodlands, meadows and steep ravines. The park offers some of the finest outdoor recreation in southwest Ohio including boating, hiking, camping and fishing.

CHECK IN:

CHECK OUT:

PARK HOURS:

DISTANCE:

FEE(S):..

WILL I RETURN? ❏ YES ❏ NO

LODGING:

WHO I WENT WITH

SIGHTS

ACTIVITIES

- ❏ ATV/OHV
- ❏ Berry Picking
- ❏ Biking
- ❏ Boating
- ❏ Canoeing
- ❏ Fishing
- ❏ Hiking
- ❏ Hunting

- ❏ Horseback Riding
- ❏ Kayaking
- ❏ Photography
- ❏ Skiing
- ❏ Skijoring
- ❏ Snowshoeing
- ❏ Snowmobiling
- ❏ Swimming

- ❏ Wildlife
- ❏ Bird Viewing
- ❏ ....
- ❏ ....
- ❏ ....
- ❏ ....
- ❏ ....
- ❏ ....

FACILITIES

- ❏ ADA
- ❏ Gift Shop
- ❏ Museum

- ❏ Visitor Center
- ❏ Picnic Sites
- ❏ Restrooms

- ❏ ....
- ❏ ....
- ❏ ....

- ❏ ....
- ❏ ....
- ❏ ....

Rating

⭐ ⭐ ⭐ ⭐ ⭐

Notes

....
....
....
....
....
....
....

PASSPORT STAMPS

CATAWBA ISLAND STATE PARK

Ottawa

DATE(S) VISITED:..

❑ SPRING ❑ SUMMER ❑ FALL ❑ WINTER

WEATHER	TEMP:
❑ ❑ ❑ ❑ ❑ ❑	

Address

4049 E Moores Dock
Rd, Port Clinton, Ohio
43452

About this State Park

Catawba Island State Park is a ten-acre (4.0 ha) public recreation area located on Lake Erie, six miles northeast of Port Clinton, Ohio. Boating, fishing and picnicking are the major activities of the park. The state park, along with the other units in Ohio's Lake Erie state parks group, was established in the early 1950s
This day-use park offers a fishing pier, launch ramps, restrooms and picnic areas can be found here. No showers and no camping. Swimming is permitted at your own risk.

CHECK IN:

CHECK OUT:

PARK HOURS:

DISTANCE:

FEE(S):..

WILL I RETURN? ❑ YES ❑ NO

LODGING:

SIGHTS

WHO I WENT WITH

ACTIVITIES

- ☐ ATV/OHV
- ☐ Berry Picking
- ☐ Biking
- ☐ Boating
- ☐ Canoeing
- ☐ Fishing
- ☐ Hiking
- ☐ Hunting

- ☐ Horseback Riding
- ☐ Kayaking
- ☐ Photography
- ☐ Skiing
- ☐ Skijoring
- ☐ Snowshoeing
- ☐ Snowmobiling
- ☐ Swimming

- ☐ Wildlife
- ☐ Bird Viewing
- ☐ ....
- ☐ ....
- ☐ ....
- ☐ ....
- ☐ ....
- ☐ ....

FACILITIES

- ☐ ADA
- ☐ Gift Shop
- ☐ Museum

- ☐ Visitor Center
- ☐ Picnic Sites
- ☐ Restrooms

- ☐ ....
- ☐ ....
- ☐ ....

- ☐ ....
- ☐ ....
- ☐ ....

Rating

★ ★ ★ ★ ★

Notes

....
....
....
....
....
....
....
....
....

PASSPORT STAMPS

COWAN LAKE STATE PARK

Clinton

DATE(S) VISITED:..

❑ SPRING ❑ SUMMER ❑ FALL ❑ WINTER

WEATHER				TEMP:	
❑	❑	❑	❑	❑	❑

Address

1750 Osborn Rd,
Wilmington, Ohio
45177

About this State Park

Cowan Lake State Park is a 1,075-acre (435 ha) public recreation area in Clinton County. It is operated by the Ohio Department of Natural Resources. The state park is open for year-round recreation and is known for a variety of birds that attract birdwatching enthusiasts to the park in southwestern Ohio.
The park offers picnic areas, pavilions, four miles of hiking trails, cottages, campsites, boating, swimming, fishing, and marina. Common game fish in Cowan Lake are muskellunge, crappie, largemouth bass, and bluegill.

CHECK IN:

CHECK OUT:

PARK HOURS:

DISTANCE:

FEE(S):..

WILL I RETURN? ❑ YES ❑ NO

LODGING:

SIGHTS

WHO I WENT WITH

ACTIVITIES

- ❏ ATV/OHV
- ❏ Berry Picking
- ❏ Biking
- ❏ Boating
- ❏ Canoeing
- ❏ Fishing
- ❏ Hiking
- ❏ Hunting

- ❏ Horseback Riding
- ❏ Kayaking
- ❏ Photography
- ❏ Skiing
- ❏ Skijoring
- ❏ Snowshoeing
- ❏ Snowmobiling
- ❏ Swimming

- ❏ Wildlife
- ❏ Bird Viewing
- ❏ ....
- ❏ ....
- ❏ ....
- ❏ ....
- ❏ ....
- ❏ ....

FACILITIES

- ❏ ADA
- ❏ Gift Shop
- ❏ Museum

- ❏ Visitor Center
- ❏ Picnic Sites
- ❏ Restrooms

- ❏ ....
- ❏ ....
- ❏ ....

- ❏ ....
- ❏ ....
- ❏ ....

Rating

⭐ ⭐ ⭐ ⭐ ⭐

Notes

....
....
....
....
....
....
....
....

PASSPORT STAMPS

DEER CREEK STATE PARK

Fayette, Pickaway

DATE(S) VISITED:...

❑ SPRING   ❑ SUMMER   ❑ FALL   ❑ WINTER

WEATHER	TEMP:

❑   ❑   ❑   ❑   ❑   ❑

Address

20635 State Park Road
20, Mt Sterling, Ohio
43143

About this State Park

Located in the heart of Ohio's agricultural country, Deer Creek
State Park is central Ohio's vacation showplace. A collage of
meadows and woodlands surround the scenic reservoir. This resort
park features a modern lodge, cottages, campground, golf course,
swimming beach and boating for outdoor enthusiasts.
The campground at Deer Creek has 232 sites. All have electricity.
Twenty-five cottages offer overnight accommodations.
The lodge at Deer Creek has 110 guest rooms, many with a
panoramic view of the lake.
A 350-acre, 18-hole golf course near the lodge is a challenge for
golfers with its 10 ponds and 52 sand traps.

CHECK IN:

CHECK OUT:

PARK HOURS:

DISTANCE:

FEE(S):..

WILL I RETURN?   ❑ YES   ❑ NO

LODGING:

WHO I WENT WITH

SIGHTS

ACTIVITIES

- ❑ ATV/OHV
- ❑ Berry Picking
- ❑ Biking
- ❑ Boating
- ❑ Canoeing
- ❑ Fishing
- ❑ Hiking
- ❑ Hunting

- ❑ Horseback Riding
- ❑ Kayaking
- ❑ Photography
- ❑ Skiing
- ❑ Skijoring
- ❑ Snowshoeing
- ❑ Snowmobiling
- ❑ Swimming

- ❑ Wildlife
- ❑ Bird Viewing
- ❑ ....
- ❑ ....
- ❑ ....
- ❑ ....
- ❑ ....
- ❑ ....

FACILITIES

- ❑ ADA
- ❑ Gift Shop
- ❑ Museum

- ❑ Visitor Center
- ❑ Picnic Sites
- ❑ Restrooms

- ❑ ....
- ❑ ....
- ❑ ....

- ❑ ....
- ❑ ....
- ❑ ....

Rating

⭐ ⭐ ⭐ ⭐ ⭐

Notes

....
....
....
....
....
....
....
....

PASSPORT STAMPS

DELAWARE STATE PARK

Delaware

DATE(S) VISITED:..

❏ SPRING   ❏ SUMMER   ❏ FALL   ❏ WINTER

WEATHER	TEMP:

❏   ❏   ❏   ❏   ❏   ❏

Address

5202 U.S. Highway 23
Delaware, Ohio   43015

About this State Park

Delaware State Park is a 1,686-acre (682 ha) public recreation area on U.S. Route 23 near the city of Delaware in Delaware County, Ohio, in the United States. It is open for year-round recreation including camping, hiking, boating, hunting, fishing, and picnicking.

Delaware State Park is open for year-round recreation. Boats with unlimited horsepower are permitted on Delaware Lake which is also open to fishing and swimming in the designated swimming area. There is a marina that sells fuel as well as fishing and boating supplies. The lake is home to a variety of game fish including largemouth and smallmouth bass, crappie, and muskellunge. Waterfowl hunting is permitted along the lake. Numerous duck blinds are awarded through a lottery system. Hunting for other game animals is permitted on the wildlife area. There are many picnic areas on the shore of the lake with tables available on a first come, first served basis.

CHECK IN:

CHECK OUT:

PARK HOURS:

DISTANCE:

FEE(S):..

WILL I RETURN?   ❏ YES   ❏ NO

LODGING:

SIGHTS

WHO I WENT WITH

ACTIVITIES

- ATV/OHV
- Berry Picking
- Biking
- Boating
- Canoeing
- Fishing
- Hiking
- Hunting

- Horseback Riding
- Kayaking
- Photography
- Skiing
- Skijoring
- Snowshoeing
- Snowmobiling
- Swimming

- Wildlife
- Bird Viewing
- ....
- ....
- ....
- ....
- ....
- ....

FACILITIES

- ADA
- Gift Shop
- Museum

- Visitor Center
- Picnic Sites
- Restrooms

- ....
- ....
- ....

- ....
- ....
- ....

Rating

★ ★ ★ ★ ★

Notes

....
....
....
....
....
....
....
....

PASSPORT STAMPS

DILLON STATE PARK

Muskingum

DATE(S) VISITED:..

❑ SPRING ❑ SUMMER ❑ FALL ❑ WINTER

Address

5265 Dillon Hills Dr
Nashport, Ohio   43830

About this State Park

Dillon Lake is a reservoir in Muskingum County. It was completed in 1961, covers 1,736 acres of water and was constructed primarily for flood control purposes. The lake was named after Moses Dillon, who purchased the land in 1803/1804.

The wooded hills and scenic valleys of the Dillon area offer a picturesque setting for outdoor adventure. Whether boating the quiet coves and inlets of the lake or hiking the forest trails, Ohio's rural hill country provides an outstanding recreational experience at Dillon State Park.

CHECK IN:

CHECK OUT:

PARK HOURS:

DISTANCE:

FEE(S):..

WILL I RETURN?   ❑ YES   ❑ NO

LODGING:

WHO I WENT WITH

SIGHTS

ACTIVITIES

❑ ATV/OHV	❑ Horseback Riding	❑ Wildlife
❑ Berry Picking	❑ Kayaking	❑ Bird Viewing
❑ Biking	❑ Photography	❑ ....
❑ Boating	❑ Skiing	❑ ....
❑ Canoeing	❑ Skijoring	❑ ....
❑ Fishing	❑ Snowshoeing	❑ ....
❑ Hiking	❑ Snowmobiling	❑ ....
❑ Hunting	❑ Swimming	❑ ....

FACILITIES

❑ ADA	❑ Visitor Center	❑	❑ ....
❑ Gift Shop	❑ Picnic Sites	❑	❑ ....
❑ Museum	❑ Restrooms	❑	❑ ....

Rating

⭐ ⭐ ⭐ ⭐ ⭐

Notes

....
....
....
....
....
....
....
....

PASSPORT STAMPS

EAST FORK STATE PARK

Clermont

DATE(S) VISITED:..

❏ SPRING ❏ SUMMER ❏ FALL ❏ WINTER

WEATHER	TEMP:
☀ ⛅ ☁ 🌧 ⛈ 🌨	
❏ ❏ ❏ ❏ ❏ ❏	

Address

3294 Elklick Rd
Bethel, Ohio 45106

About this State Park

East Fork State Park is 4,870-acre (1,970 ha) public recreation area located around the East Fork of the Little Miami River in Clermont County, twenty miles (32 km) southeast of central Cincinnati. It has camping, hiking, swimming, and boating opportunities. The state park has hosted junior and collegiate rowing races, including the US Rowing Youth National Championships.[3] The park's main feature is William H. Harsha Lake, a 2,107-acre (853 ha) reservoir created in 1978. The lake's large earthen dam and smaller saddle dams are operated by the U.S. Army Corps of Engineers.
Fish found in the lake include largemouth bass, smallmouth bass, Kentucky spotted bass, bluegill, white crappie, black crappie, channel catfish, flathead catfish, bigmouth buffalofish, carp, and hybrid striped bass.

CHECK IN:

CHECK OUT:

PARK HOURS:

DISTANCE:

FEE(S):...

WILL I RETURN?   ❏ YES   ❏ NO

LODGING:

SIGHTS

WHO I WENT WITH

ACTIVITIES

❑ ATV/OHV	❑ Horseback Riding	❑ Wildlife
❑ Berry Picking	❑ Kayaking	❑ Bird Viewing
❑ Biking	❑ Photography	❑ ....
❑ Boating	❑ Skiing	❑ ....
❑ Canoeing	❑ Skijoring	❑ ....
❑ Fishing	❑ Snowshoeing	❑ ....
❑ Hiking	❑ Snowmobiling	❑ ....
❑ Hunting	❑ Swimming	❑ ....

FACILITIES

❑ ADA	❑ Visitor Center	❑	❑ ....
❑ Gift Shop	❑ Picnic Sites	❑	❑ ....
❑ Museum	❑ Restrooms	❑	❑ ....

Rating

⭐ ⭐ ⭐ ⭐ ⭐

Notes

....
....
....
....
....
....
....
....

PASSPORT STAMPS

EAST HARBOR STATE PARK

Ottawa

DATE(S) VISITED:..

❏ SPRING   ❏ SUMMER   ❏ FALL   ❏ WINTER

WEATHER			TEMP:		
❏	❏	❏	❏	❏	❏

Address

Lakeside Marblehead,
Ohio   43440

About this State Park

East Harbor State Park is a public recreation area located eight miles (13 km) northwest of Sandusky, Ohio on the shores of Lake Erie. The state park includes beach, campground, marina, and wetland wildlife preserve areas. The park offers swimming, boating and fishing, ten miles (16 km) of multi-use trails, picnicking, hunting, and disc golf.

A thin stretch of sand beach juts northward into the waters of Lake Erie, separating Middle Harbor from the lake. Part of this beach was damaged in 1972 by a storm washing away a large section of the two-mile (3 km) beach. The current beach is a much smaller area to the north of the park, where swimming is permitted. Four segmented offshore breakwaters have been constructed on the northern section of beach, to sustain what is left of the sandy shoreline.

CHECK IN:

CHECK OUT:

PARK HOURS:

DISTANCE:

FEE(S):..

WILL I RETURN?   ❏ YES   ❏ NO

LODGING:

SIGHTS

WHO I WENT WITH

ACTIVITIES

- ☐ ATV/OHV
- ☐ Berry Picking
- ☐ Biking
- ☐ Boating
- ☐ Canoeing
- ☐ Fishing
- ☐ Hiking
- ☐ Hunting

- ☐ Horseback Riding
- ☐ Kayaking
- ☐ Photography
- ☐ Skiing
- ☐ Skijoring
- ☐ Snowshoeing
- ☐ Snowmobiling
- ☐ Swimming

- ☐ Wildlife
- ☐ Bird Viewing
- ☐ ....
- ☐ ....
- ☐ ....
- ☐ ....
- ☐ ....
- ☐ ....

FACILITIES

- ☐ ADA
- ☐ Gift Shop
- ☐ Museum

- ☐ Visitor Center
- ☐ Picnic Sites
- ☐ Restrooms

- ☐ ....
- ☐ ....
- ☐ ....

- ☐ ....
- ☐ ....
- ☐ ....

Rating

★ ★ ★ ★ ★

Notes

....
....
....
....
....
....
....
....

PASSPORT STAMPS

FINDLEY STATE PARK

Lorain

DATE(S) VISITED:..

❑ SPRING   ❑ SUMMER   ❑ FALL   ❑ WINTER

WEATHER			TEMP:		
☀	☁	☁	🌧	🌧	🌨
❑	❑	❑	❑	❑	❑

Address

25381 OH-58,
Wellington, Ohio
44090

About this State Park

Once a state forest, Findley State Park is heavily wooded with stately pines and various hardwoods. The scenic hiking trails allow nature lovers to view spectacular wildflowers and observe wildlife. The fields, forests and quiet waters offer a peaceful refuge for visitors. Findley's campground offers 272 non-electric sites in both sunny and shaded areas. The campground features showers, flush toilets, laundry facilities, dump station, game room and a fully stocked camp store. Pet camping is permitted on designated sites. Three rustic camper cabins complete with cots, dining fly and multi-level picnic grill can be rented during the summer months by reservation. A recreation area with sand volleyball, a basketball court and two horseshoe pits are also available for camper use.

CHECK IN:

CHECK OUT:

PARK HOURS:

DISTANCE:

FEE(S):..

WILL I RETURN?   ❑ YES   ❑ NO

LODGING:

SIGHTS

WHO I WENT WITH

ACTIVITIES

❑ ATV/OHV	❑ Horseback Riding	❑ Wildlife
❑ Berry Picking	❑ Kayaking	❑ Bird Viewing
❑ Biking	❑ Photography	❑ ....
❑ Boating	❑ Skiing	❑ ....
❑ Canoeing	❑ Skijoring	❑ ....
❑ Fishing	❑ Snowshoeing	❑ ....
❑ Hiking	❑ Snowmobiling	❑ ....
❑ Hunting	❑ Swimming	❑ ....

FACILITIES

❑ ADA	❑ Visitor Center	❑	❑ ....
❑ Gift Shop	❑ Picnic Sites	❑	❑ ....
❑ Museum	❑ Restrooms	❑	❑ ....

Rating

⭐ ⭐ ⭐ ⭐ ⭐

Notes

....
....
....
....
....
....
....
....

PASSPORT STAMPS

FORKED RUN STATE PARK

Meigs

DATE(S) VISITED:...

❑ SPRING   ❑ SUMMER   ❑ FALL   ❑ WINTER

WEATHER			TEMP:		
☀	☁	☁	☁	☁	☁
❑	❑	❑	❑	❑	❑

Address

63300 OH-124
Reedsville,
Ohio 45772

About this State Park

Forked Run State Park is a public recreation area located three miles (4.8 km) south of Reedsville in eastern Meigs County. The state park's area is 791 acres (320 ha), while the lake covers 102 acres (41 ha).The name is pronounced with two syllables for "Forked". It fronts on Ohio State Route 124. The park borders the Shade River State Forest, from which it was created in 1951. The dam was created in 1952, when the park was opened to the public.
Park features include campground, rustic cabins, picnic facilities, hiking trails, swimming beach, boat ramps, and disc golf course. It also is located close to an Ohio River boat ramp, so the campground also serves Ohio River boaters.

CHECK IN:

CHECK OUT:

PARK HOURS:

DISTANCE:

FEE(S):...

WILL I RETURN?   ❑ YES   ❑ NO

LODGING:

SIGHTS

WHO I WENT WITH

ACTIVITIES

- ❑ ATV/OHV
- ❑ Berry Picking
- ❑ Biking
- ❑ Boating
- ❑ Canoeing
- ❑ Fishing
- ❑ Hiking
- ❑ Hunting

- ❑ Horseback Riding
- ❑ Kayaking
- ❑ Photography
- ❑ Skiing
- ❑ Skijoring
- ❑ Snowshoeing
- ❑ Snowmobiling
- ❑ Swimming

- ❑ Wildlife
- ❑ Bird Viewing
- ❑ ....
- ❑ ....
- ❑ ....
- ❑ ....
- ❑ ....
- ❑ ....

FACILITIES

- ❑ ADA
- ❑ Gift Shop
- ❑ Museum

- ❑ Visitor Center
- ❑ Picnic Sites
- ❑ Restrooms

- ❑ ....
- ❑ ....
- ❑ ....

- ❑ ....
- ❑ ....
- ❑ ....

Rating

⭐ ⭐ ⭐ ⭐ ⭐

Notes

....
....
....
....
....
....
....
....

PASSPORT STAMPS

GENEVA STATE PARK

Ashtabula

DATE(S) VISITED:...

❏ SPRING   ❏ SUMMER   ❏ FALL   ❏ WINTER

WEATHER	TEMP:
☀ ❏ ⛅ ❏ ☁ ❏ 🌧 ❏ ⛈ ❏ 🌨 ❏	

Address

4499 Padanarum Rd
Geneva, Ohio 44041-8172

About this State Park

Geneva State Park's cottage replacement is underway. Twelve cottages and an enclosed group shelterhouse will be available late this summer. Located on Ohio's northeastern shoreline, Geneva State Park reflects the character and charisma of Lake Erie. The shimmering expanse of the lake lures vacationers who enjoy fishing and boating. Swimmers rejoice in the beautiful sand beach while nature enthusiasts retreat to the park's freshwater marshes and estuaries associated with the lake.

CHECK IN:

CHECK OUT:

PARK HOURS:

DISTANCE:

FEE(S):..

WILL I RETURN?   ❏ YES   ❏ NO

LODGING:

WHO I WENT WITH

SIGHTS

ACTIVITIES

- [ ] ATV/OHV
- [ ] Berry Picking
- [ ] Biking
- [ ] Boating
- [ ] Canoeing
- [ ] Fishing
- [ ] Hiking
- [ ] Hunting

- [ ] Horseback Riding
- [ ] Kayaking
- [ ] Photography
- [ ] Skiing
- [ ] Skijoring
- [ ] Snowshoeing
- [ ] Snowmobiling
- [ ] Swimming

- [ ] Wildlife
- [ ] Bird Viewing
- [ ] ....
- [ ] ....
- [ ] ....
- [ ] ....
- [ ] ....
- [ ] ....

FACILITIES

- [ ] ADA
- [ ] Gift Shop
- [ ] Museum

- [ ] Visitor Center
- [ ] Picnic Sites
- [ ] Restrooms

- [ ] ....
- [ ] ....
- [ ] ....

- [ ] ....
- [ ] ....
- [ ] ....

Rating

★ ★ ★ ★ ★

Notes

....
....
....
....
....
....
....
....

PASSPORT STAMPS

GRAND LAKE ST. MARYS STATE PARK

Auglaize

DATE(S) VISITED:..

❏ SPRING   ❏ SUMMER   ❏ FALL   ❏ WINTER

WEATHER			TEMP:		
☀	☁	☁	☁	☁	☁
❏	❏	❏	❏	❏	❏

Address

834 Edgewater Dr
St Marys, Ohio   45885

About this State Park

Grand Lake St. Marys State Park is a public recreation area located on 13,500-acre (5,500 ha) Grand Lake in Mercer and Auglaize counties, Grand Lake is the largest inland lake in Ohio in terms of area, but is shallow, with an average depth of only 5–7 feet (1.5–2.1 m). The state park is open for year-round recreation, including boating, fishing, swimming and hunting. The park consists of the lake and park facilities scattered all around the shore intermingled with private property and a facility operated by Wright State University. It is west of St. Marys, and south-east of Celina, 23 miles (37 km) south-west of Lima in the north-western part of Ohio.

CHECK IN:

CHECK OUT:

PARK HOURS:

DISTANCE:

FEE(S):..

WILL I RETURN?   ❏ YES   ❏ NO

LODGING:

SIGHTS

WHO I WENT WITH

ACTIVITIES

❑ ATV/OHV	❑ Horseback Riding	❑ Wildlife
❑ Berry Picking	❑ Kayaking	❑ Bird Viewing
❑ Biking	❑ Photography	❑ ....
❑ Boating	❑ Skiing	❑ ....
❑ Canoeing	❑ Skijoring	❑ ....
❑ Fishing	❑ Snowshoeing	❑ ....
❑ Hiking	❑ Snowmobiling	❑ ....
❑ Hunting	❑ Swimming	❑ ....

FACILITIES

❑ ADA	❑ Visitor Center	❑	❑ ....
❑ Gift Shop	❑ Picnic Sites	❑	❑ ....
❑ Museum	❑ Restrooms	❑	❑ ....

Rating

⭐ ⭐ ⭐ ⭐ ⭐

Notes

....
....
....
....
....
....
....
....

PASSPORT STAMPS

GREAT SEAL STATE PARK

Ross

DATE(S) VISITED:...

❏ SPRING　　❏ SUMMER　　❏ FALL　　❏ WINTER

WEATHER	TEMP:

❏　❏　❏　❏　❏　❏

Address

4908 Marietta Rd
Chillicothe,
Ohio   45601

About this State Park

Great Seal State Park is dedicated to the wilderness spirit of Ohio. The history of the Shawnee nation and Ohio's early statehood is centered in these rugged hills. Challenging trails take visitors to scenic vistas of distant ridgetops and the Scioto Valley below. These very hills are depicted on the Great Seal of the State of Ohio, from which the park gets its name.
A 15-site campground offers pressurized water, vault latrines and a shelterhouse. The campground is scenically located adjacent to Sugarloaf Mountain, offering a view of the Scioto Valley below. Campers with pets are permitted.

CHECK IN:

CHECK OUT:

PARK HOURS:

DISTANCE:

FEE(S):...

WILL I RETURN?　❏ YES　　❏ NO

LODGING:

SIGHTS

WHO I WENT WITH

ACTIVITIES

- ❑ ATV/OHV
- ❑ Berry Picking
- ❑ Biking
- ❑ Boating
- ❑ Canoeing
- ❑ Fishing
- ❑ Hiking
- ❑ Hunting

- ❑ Horseback Riding
- ❑ Kayaking
- ❑ Photography
- ❑ Skiing
- ❑ Skijoring
- ❑ Snowshoeing
- ❑ Snowmobiling
- ❑ Swimming

- ❑ Wildlife
- ❑ Bird Viewing
- ❑ ....
- ❑ ....
- ❑ ....
- ❑ ....
- ❑ ....
- ❑ ....

FACILITIES

- ❑ ADA
- ❑ Gift Shop
- ❑ Museum

- ❑ Visitor Center
- ❑ Picnic Sites
- ❑ Restrooms

- ❑ ....
- ❑ ....
- ❑ ....

- ❑ ....
- ❑ ....
- ❑ ....

Rating

⭐ ⭐ ⭐ ⭐ ⭐

Notes

....
....
....
....
....
....
....
....

PASSPORT STAMPS

GUILFORD LAKE STATE PARK

Columbiana

DATE(S) VISITED:...

❏ SPRING ❏ SUMMER ❏ FALL ❏ WINTER

WEATHER					
❏	❏	❏	❏	❏	❏

TEMP:

Address

6835 E Lake Rd
Lisbon, Ohio   44432

About this State Park

Guilford Lake State Park is a quiet fishing lake located in northeastern Ohio on the west fork of the Little Beaver Creek. The gentle rolling terrain of the area offers a serene escape for park visitors year round.
There is a camping area with 42 electric sites located in an old pine plantation on the northeast corner of the lake, providing shady and sunny areas. A play area, fishing dock, drinking water, showers, flush toilets, picnic tables and fire-rings are provided.

CHECK IN:

CHECK OUT:

PARK HOURS:

DISTANCE:

FEE(S):..

WILL I RETURN?   ❏ YES   ❏ NO

LODGING:

WHO I WENT WITH

SIGHTS

ACTIVITIES

- ❏ ATV/OHV
- ❏ Berry Picking
- ❏ Biking
- ❏ Boating
- ❏ Canoeing
- ❏ Fishing
- ❏ Hiking
- ❏ Hunting

- ❏ Horseback Riding
- ❏ Kayaking
- ❏ Photography
- ❏ Skiing
- ❏ Skijoring
- ❏ Snowshoeing
- ❏ Snowmobiling
- ❏ Swimming

- ❏ Wildlife
- ❏ Bird Viewing
- ❏ ....
- ❏ ....
- ❏ ....
- ❏ ....
- ❏ ....
- ❏ ....

FACILITIES

- ❏ ADA
- ❏ Gift Shop
- ❏ Museum

- ❏ Visitor Center
- ❏ Picnic Sites
- ❏ Restrooms

- ❏ ....
- ❏ ....
- ❏ ....

- ❏ ....
- ❏ ....
- ❏ ....

Rating

⭐ ⭐ ⭐ ⭐ ⭐

Notes

....
....
....
....
....
....
....
....

PASSPORT STAMPS

HARRISON LAKE STATE PARK

Fulton

DATE(S) VISITED:..

❏ SPRING   ❏ SUMMER   ❏ FALL   ❏ WINTER

WEATHER			TEMP:		
❏	❏	❏	❏	❏	❏

Address

26246 Harrison Lake Rd, Fayette, Ohio 43521

About this State Park

Harrison Lake State Park is a 142-acre (57 ha) public recreation area located three miles (4.8 km) southwest of Fayette. The park surrounds 95-acre (38 ha) Harrison Lake, which has a maximum depth of fifteen feet near the dam and provides a habitat for bluegill, channel catfish, largemouth bass, white crappie, and bullhead. The state park includes a 3.5-mile (5.6 km) hiking trail around the lake, swimming beach, and camping area.

CHECK IN:

CHECK OUT:

PARK HOURS:

DISTANCE:

FEE(S):..

WILL I RETURN?   ❏ YES   ❏ NO

LODGING:

SIGHTS

WHO I WENT WITH

ACTIVITIES

- ❑ ATV/OHV
- ❑ Berry Picking
- ❑ Biking
- ❑ Boating
- ❑ Canoeing
- ❑ Fishing
- ❑ Hiking
- ❑ Hunting

- ❑ Horseback Riding
- ❑ Kayaking
- ❑ Photography
- ❑ Skiing
- ❑ Skijoring
- ❑ Snowshoeing
- ❑ Snowmobiling
- ❑ Swimming

- ❑ Wildlife
- ❑ Bird Viewing
- ❑ ....
- ❑ ....
- ❑ ....
- ❑ ....
- ❑ ....
- ❑ ....

FACILITIES

- ❑ ADA
- ❑ Gift Shop
- ❑ Museum

- ❑ Visitor Center
- ❑ Picnic Sites
- ❑ Restrooms

- ❑ ....
- ❑ ....
- ❑ ....

- ❑ ....
- ❑ ....
- ❑ ....

Rating

⭐ ⭐ ⭐ ⭐ ⭐

Notes

....
....
....
....
....
....
....
....

PASSPORT STAMPS

HEADLANDS BEACH STATE PARK

Lake

DATE(S) VISITED:..

❏ SPRING   ❏ SUMMER   ❏ FALL   ❏ WINTER

WEATHER				TEMP:	
☀	❄☁	☁	🌧	🌧	🌨
❏	❏	❏	❏	❏	❏

About this State Park

Headlands Beach State Park is a public beach in Mentor and Painesville Township. It is the longest natural beach in Ohio and attracts two million visitors annually. The breakwall at the eastern end of the park, frequented by fishermen, is surmounted by the Fairport Harbor West Breakwater Light. The park features a 35-acre beach for sunbathing, swimming, and beach glass hunting along with picnicking facilities and seasonal concessionaire.
the area is home to many plant species typically found only along the Atlantic Coast.

CHECK IN:

CHECK OUT:

PARK HOURS:

DISTANCE:

FEE(S):..

WILL I RETURN?   ❏ YES   ❏ NO

LODGING:

SIGHTS

WHO I WENT WITH

ACTIVITIES

- ❑ ATV/OHV
- ❑ Berry Picking
- ❑ Biking
- ❑ Boating
- ❑ Canoeing
- ❑ Fishing
- ❑ Hiking
- ❑ Hunting

- ❑ Horseback Riding
- ❑ Kayaking
- ❑ Photography
- ❑ Skiing
- ❑ Skijoring
- ❑ Snowshoeing
- ❑ Snowmobiling
- ❑ Swimming

- ❑ Wildlife
- ❑ Bird Viewing
- ❑ ....
- ❑ ....
- ❑ ....
- ❑ ....
- ❑ ....
- ❑ ....

FACILITIES

- ❑ ADA
- ❑ Gift Shop
- ❑ Museum

- ❑ Visitor Center
- ❑ Picnic Sites
- ❑ Restrooms

- ❑ ....
- ❑ ....
- ❑ ....

- ❑ ....
- ❑ ....
- ❑ ....

Rating

⭐ ⭐ ⭐ ⭐ ⭐

Notes

....
....
....
....
....
....
....
....

PASSPORT STAMPS

HOCKING HILLS STATE PARK

Hocking

DATE(S) VISITED:..

❏ SPRING   ❏ SUMMER   ❏ FALL   ❏ WINTER

WEATHER			TEMP:		
❏	❏	❏	❏	❏	❏

Address

19852 OH-664, Logan, Ohio   43138

About this State Park

Hocking Hills State Park is a state park in the Hocking Hills region of Hocking County. In some areas the park adjoins the Hocking State Forest. Within the park are over 25 miles (40 km) of hiking trails, rock formations, waterfalls, and recess caves. The trails are open from dawn to dusk, all year round, including holidays.

The park contains seven separate hiking areas: Ash Cave, Cantwell Cliffs, Cedar Falls, Conkle's Hollow (nature preserve), Old Man's Cave, Rock House and Hemlock Bridge Trail to Whispering Cave.

CHECK IN:

CHECK OUT:

PARK HOURS:

DISTANCE:

FEE(S):..

WILL I RETURN?   ❏ YES   ❏ NO

LODGING:

SIGHTS

WHO I WENT WITH

ACTIVITIES

- ❏ ATV/OHV
- ❏ Berry Picking
- ❏ Biking
- ❏ Boating
- ❏ Canoeing
- ❏ Fishing
- ❏ Hiking
- ❏ Hunting

- ❏ Horseback Riding
- ❏ Kayaking
- ❏ Photography
- ❏ Skiing
- ❏ Skijoring
- ❏ Snowshoeing
- ❏ Snowmobiling
- ❏ Swimming

- ❏ Wildlife
- ❏ Bird Viewing
- ❏ ....
- ❏ ....
- ❏ ....
- ❏ ....
- ❏ ....
- ❏ ....

FACILITIES

- ❏ ADA
- ❏ Gift Shop
- ❏ Museum

- ❏ Visitor Center
- ❏ Picnic Sites
- ❏ Restrooms

- ❏ ....
- ❏ ....
- ❏ ....

- ❏ ....
- ❏ ....
- ❏ ....

Rating

⭐ ⭐ ⭐ ⭐ ⭐

Notes

....
....
....
....
....
....
....
....

PASSPORT STAMPS

HUESTON WOODS STATE PARK

Butler, Preble

DATE(S) VISITED:...

❑ SPRING ❑ SUMMER ❑ FALL ❑ WINTER

WEATHER	TEMP:
☀ ❄ ☁ ☁ ☁ ☁	
❑ ❑ ❑ ❑ ❑ ❑	

Address

College Corner, Ohio
45003

About this State Park

Hueston Woods State Park is a state park located in Butler and Preble counties of the U.S. state of Ohio, about five miles (8 km) northeast of Oxford in the southwestern part of the state. The park lies in Oxford Township, Butler County, and Israel Township, Preble County. It has nearly 3,000 acres (1,200 ha), including a man-made lake of 625 acres (253 ha). The park's beech-maple climax forest has been designated a National Natural Landmark. The park offers boating, camping, fishing, swimming, 12 miles (19 km) of hiking trails, 18 miles (29 km) of bridal trails, 20 miles (32 km) of mountain biking trails, cabins, 96-room lodge, and golf course.

CHECK IN:

CHECK OUT:

PARK HOURS:

DISTANCE:

FEE(S):...

WILL I RETURN? ❑ YES ❑ NO

LODGING:

SIGHTS

WHO I WENT WITH

ACTIVITIES

❑ ATV/OHV	❑ Horseback Riding	❑ Wildlife
❑ Berry Picking	❑ Kayaking	❑ Bird Viewing
❑ Biking	❑ Photography	❑ ....
❑ Boating	❑ Skiing	❑ ....
❑ Canoeing	❑ Skijoring	❑ ....
❑ Fishing	❑ Snowshoeing	❑ ....
❑ Hiking	❑ Snowmobiling	❑ ....
❑ Hunting	❑ Swimming	❑ ....

FACILITIES

❑ ADA	❑ Visitor Center	❑	❑ ....
❑ Gift Shop	❑ Picnic Sites	❑	❑ ....
❑ Museum	❑ Restrooms	❑	❑ ....

Rating

★ ★ ★ ★ ★

Notes

....
....
....
....
....
....
....
....

PASSPORT STAMPS

INDEPENDENCE DAM STATE PARK

Defiance

DATE(S) VISITED:..

❑ SPRING   ❑ SUMMER   ❑ FALL   ❑ WINTER

WEATHER		TEMP:

❑   ❑   ❑   ❑   ❑   ❑

Address

27722 County Rd 424,
Defiance, Ohio   43512

About this State Park

Independence Dam State Park is a 591-acre (239 ha) public recreation area located on the banks of the Maumee River three miles east of Defiance in Defiance County, Ohio, United States. The state park features ruins of the Miami and Erie Canal. Recreational features include boating, fishing, hiking, picnicking, and primitive camping. The former towpath for the Miami and Erie Canal is used for hiking and biking. The park features a four-lane boat ramp and hand-launches providing access to the Maumee River, which offers water skiing, paddling opportunities, and fishing for northern pike, crappie, walleye, smallmouth bass, and catfish. Picnic tables sit along the river bank. A primitive tent campground was added in 2019.

CHECK IN:

CHECK OUT:

PARK HOURS:

DISTANCE:

FEE(S):...

WILL I RETURN?   ❑ YES   ❑ NO

LODGING:

SIGHTS

WHO I WENT WITH

ACTIVITIES

❑ ATV/OHV	❑ Horseback Riding	❑ Wildlife
❑ Berry Picking	❑ Kayaking	❑ Bird Viewing
❑ Biking	❑ Photography	❑ ....
❑ Boating	❑ Skiing	❑ ....
❑ Canoeing	❑ Skijoring	❑ ....
❑ Fishing	❑ Snowshoeing	❑ ....
❑ Hiking	❑ Snowmobiling	❑ ....
❑ Hunting	❑ Swimming	❑ ....

FACILITIES

❑ ADA	❑ Visitor Center	❑	❑ ....
❑ Gift Shop	❑ Picnic Sites	❑	❑ ....
❑ Museum	❑ Restrooms	❑	❑ ....

Rating

★ ★ ★ ★ ★

Notes

....
....
....
....
....
....
....

PASSPORT STAMPS

INDIAN LAKE STATE PARK

Logan

DATE(S) VISITED:...

❑ SPRING   ❑ SUMMER   ❑ FALL   ❑ WINTER

WEATHER						TEMP:
❑	❑	❑	❑	❑	❑	

Address

13156 OH-235,
Lakeview, Ohio   43331

About this State Park

Indian Lake offers a diversity of water-related recreational opportunities. Boating, fishing, skiing and camping are highlights of this multi-use park.
There are 443 family campsites suitable for tents or trailers on the northwest section of the lakeshore. The scenic campground offers electric hookups for most sites, heated shower houses, flush toilets, laundry facility and camp commissary. A beach, boat ramp and boat docks are provided for exclusive camper use. A limited number of pet camping sites are available. The park's group camp area may be reserved by advanced registration. Twenty boat camping spaces are also available.

CHECK IN:

CHECK OUT:

PARK HOURS:

DISTANCE:

FEE(S):..

WILL I RETURN?   ❑ YES   ❑ NO

LODGING:

SIGHTS

WHO I WENT WITH

ACTIVITIES

- ❑ ATV/OHV
- ❑ Berry Picking
- ❑ Biking
- ❑ Boating
- ❑ Canoeing
- ❑ Fishing
- ❑ Hiking
- ❑ Hunting

- ❑ Horseback Riding
- ❑ Kayaking
- ❑ Photography
- ❑ Skiing
- ❑ Skijoring
- ❑ Snowshoeing
- ❑ Snowmobiling
- ❑ Swimming

- ❑ Wildlife
- ❑ Bird Viewing
- ❑ ....
- ❑ ....
- ❑ ....
- ❑ ....
- ❑ ....
- ❑ ....

FACILITIES

- ❑ ADA
- ❑ Gift Shop
- ❑ Museum

- ❑ Visitor Center
- ❑ Picnic Sites
- ❑ Restrooms

- ❑ ....
- ❑ ....
- ❑ ....

- ❑ ....
- ❑ ....
- ❑ ....

Rating

★ ★ ★ ★ ★

Notes

....
....
....
....
....
....
....
....

PASSPORT STAMPS

JACKSON LAKE STATE PARK

Jackson

DATE(S) VISITED:...

❏ SPRING ❏ SUMMER ❏ FALL ❏ WINTER

WEATHER	TEMP:
☀ ❄☁ ☁ ☁ ☁ ☁	
❏ ❏ ❏ ❏ ❏ ❏	

Address

921 Tommy Been Rd
Oak Hill, Ohio   45656

About this State Park

Although relatively small, Jackson Lake State Park boasts acres of some of the most scenic country in Ohio. The park's serene lake is a focal point for excellent fishing and provides the ideal setting for a peaceful retreat.
A small campground with 34 electric sites has open sites close to the beach. Campers with pets are permitted in designated areas.

CHECK IN:

CHECK OUT:

PARK HOURS:

DISTANCE:

FEE(S):...

WILL I RETURN?   ❏ YES   ❏ NO

LODGING:

SIGHTS

WHO I WENT WITH

ACTIVITIES

- ❑ ATV/OHV
- ❑ Berry Picking
- ❑ Biking
- ❑ Boating
- ❑ Canoeing
- ❑ Fishing
- ❑ Hiking
- ❑ Hunting

- ❑ Horseback Riding
- ❑ Kayaking
- ❑ Photography
- ❑ Skiing
- ❑ Skijoring
- ❑ Snowshoeing
- ❑ Snowmobiling
- ❑ Swimming

- ❑ Wildlife
- ❑ Bird Viewing
- ❑ ....
- ❑ ....
- ❑ ....
- ❑ ....
- ❑ ....
- ❑ ....

FACILITIES

- ❑ ADA
- ❑ Gift Shop
- ❑ Museum

- ❑ Visitor Center
- ❑ Picnic Sites
- ❑ Restrooms

- ❑ ....
- ❑ ....
- ❑ ....

- ❑ ....
- ❑ ....
- ❑ ....

Rating

⭐ ⭐ ⭐ ⭐ ⭐

Notes

....
....
....
....
....
....
....
....

PASSPORT STAMPS

JEFFERSON LAKE STATE PARK

Jefferson

DATE(S) VISITED:...

❑ SPRING   ❑ SUMMER   ❑ FALL   ❑ WINTER

WEATHER			TEMP:		
☀	☁	☁	☁	☁	☁
❑	❑	❑	❑	❑	❑

Address

501 Township Rd 261A,
Richmond, Ohio
43944

About this State Park

The sandstone hills of Jefferson County are part of the Appalachian Highlands which envelop the southeastern part of Ohio. In the sandstone bedrock can be found layers of coal which were formed by decaying swamp vegetation millions of years ago during the Pennsylvanian geologic period.

There is a family camping area suitable for tents and trailers offering 97 non-electric sites. Latrines water fountains, picnic tables and fire rings are provided.

CHECK IN:

CHECK OUT:

PARK HOURS:

DISTANCE:

FEE(S):...

WILL I RETURN?   ❑ YES   ❑ NO

LODGING:

SIGHTS

WHO I WENT WITH

ACTIVITIES

- ❏ ATV/OHV
- ❏ Berry Picking
- ❏ Biking
- ❏ Boating
- ❏ Canoeing
- ❏ Fishing
- ❏ Hiking
- ❏ Hunting

- ❏ Horseback Riding
- ❏ Kayaking
- ❏ Photography
- ❏ Skiing
- ❏ Skijoring
- ❏ Snowshoeing
- ❏ Snowmobiling
- ❏ Swimming

- ❏ Wildlife
- ❏ Bird Viewing
- ❏ ....
- ❏ ....
- ❏ ....
- ❏ ....
- ❏ ....
- ❏ ....

FACILITIES

- ❏ ADA
- ❏ Gift Shop
- ❏ Museum

- ❏ Visitor Center
- ❏ Picnic Sites
- ❏ Restrooms

- ❏ ....
- ❏ ....
- ❏ ....

- ❏ ....
- ❏ ....
- ❏ ....

Rating

★ ★ ★ ★ ★

Notes

....
....
....
....
....
....
....

PASSPORT STAMPS

JOHN BRYAN STATE PARK

Greene

DATE(S) VISITED:...

❏ SPRING   ❏ SUMMER   ❏ FALL   ❏ WINTER

WEATHER	TEMP:
☀ ❏ ⛅ ❏ ☁ ❏ 🌧 ❏ 🌧 ❏ 🌨 ❏	

Address

3790 OH-370, Yellow
Springs, Ohio   45387

About this State Park

John Bryan State Park is a 752-acre (304 ha) Ohio state park in
Greene County. The park surrounds Clifton Gorge, a deep cut of
the Little Miami River between Yellow Springs and Clifton. The
park contains a campground, and hiking and biking trails. The
park also abuts the Clifton Gorge State Nature Preserve and Glen
Helen Nature Preserve.
John Bryan is the most scenic state park in western Ohio. The park
contains a remarkable limestone gorge cut by the Little Miami
River which is designated as a state and national scenic river. A
portion of the gorge itself is designated as a national natural
landmark.

CHECK IN:

CHECK OUT:

PARK HOURS:

DISTANCE:

FEE(S):...

WILL I RETURN?   ❏ YES   ❏ NO

LODGING:

SIGHTS

WHO I WENT WITH

ACTIVITIES

- ❑ ATV/OHV
- ❑ Berry Picking
- ❑ Biking
- ❑ Boating
- ❑ Canoeing
- ❑ Fishing
- ❑ Hiking
- ❑ Hunting
- ❑ Horseback Riding
- ❑ Kayaking
- ❑ Photography
- ❑ Skiing
- ❑ Skijoring
- ❑ Snowshoeing
- ❑ Snowmobiling
- ❑ Swimming
- ❑ Wildlife
- ❑ Bird Viewing
- ❑ ....
- ❑ ....
- ❑ ....
- ❑ ....
- ❑ ....
- ❑ ....

FACILITIES

- ❑ ADA
- ❑ Gift Shop
- ❑ Museum
- ❑ Visitor Center
- ❑ Picnic Sites
- ❑ Restrooms
- ❑ ....
- ❑ ....
- ❑ ....
- ❑ ....
- ❑ ....
- ❑ ....

Rating

⭐ ⭐ ⭐ ⭐ ⭐

Notes

....
....
....
....
....
....
....
....

PASSPORT STAMPS

KELLEYS ISLAND STATE PARK

Erie

DATE(S) VISITED:..

❑ SPRING ❑ SUMMER ❑ FALL ❑ WINTER

WEATHER			TEMP:	
☀ ❄☁	☁	☁	☁	☁
❑	❑	❑	❑	❑

Address

920 Division St
Kelleys Island,
Ohio 43438

About this State Park

Kelleys Island State Park is a public recreation area occupying one-quarter of Kelleys Island, an island in Lake Erie located 13 miles (21 km) northeast of Port Clinton. The state park's 677 acres (274 ha) include six miles (9.7 km) of hiking trails, ruins of lime kilns and quarrying operations, sand beach, and campground. The park was established in 1956. The park cooperates with other agencies to manage the adjoining Glacial Grooves State Memorial, a set of rare glacial grooves, North Shore Alvar State Natural Area, a rare alvar habitat, and the North Pond State Nature Preserve, a lake embayment usually separated from the lake by a sand bar.

The family campground contains 45 non-electric and 84 electric sites, Six miles of hiking trails lead to scenic vistas, historic sites and two nature preserves, North Pond Nature Preserve, and the North Shore Nature Preserve, offering excellent locations for watching wildlife. Picnic areas, a picnic shelter, launch ramps, fishing access areas and a 100-foot swimming beach are also available. Limited hunting is permitted in designated areas of the park.

CHECK IN:

CHECK OUT:

PARK HOURS:

DISTANCE:

FEE(S):...

WILL I RETURN? ❑ YES ❑ NO

LODGING:

WHO I WENT WITH

SIGHTS

ACTIVITIES

- ❑ ATV/OHV
- ❑ Berry Picking
- ❑ Biking
- ❑ Boating
- ❑ Canoeing
- ❑ Fishing
- ❑ Hiking
- ❑ Hunting

- ❑ Horseback Riding
- ❑ Kayaking
- ❑ Photography
- ❑ Skiing
- ❑ Skijoring
- ❑ Snowshoeing
- ❑ Snowmobiling
- ❑ Swimming

- ❑ Wildlife
- ❑ Bird Viewing
- ❑ ....
- ❑ ....
- ❑ ....
- ❑ ....
- ❑ ....
- ❑ ....

FACILITIES

- ❑ ADA
- ❑ Gift Shop
- ❑ Museum

- ❑ Visitor Center
- ❑ Picnic Sites
- ❑ Restrooms

- ❑ ....
- ❑ ....
- ❑ ....

- ❑ ....
- ❑ ....
- ❑ ....

Rating

★ ★ ★ ★ ★

Notes

....

....

....

....

....

....

....

....

PASSPORT STAMPS

KISER LAKE STATE PARK

Champaign

DATE(S) VISITED:..

❑ SPRING   ❑ SUMMER   ❑ FALL   ❑ WINTER

WEATHER		TEMP:			
☀	❄☁	☁	☁	☁	☁
❑	❑	❑	❑	❑	❑

Address

4889 OH-235, Conover,
Ohio   45317

About this State Park

Kiser Lake State Park is a public recreation area in Champaign County, Ohio, located four miles (6.4 km) northwest of St. Paris and 34 miles (55 km) north of Dayton.[2] The 531-acre (215 ha) state park includes 396-acre (160 ha) Kiser Lake, for which it was named, and the 51-acre (21 ha) Kiser Lake Wetlands State Nature Preserve.
In addition to being a popular fishing location, ODNR maintains one boat ramp, four smaller launch areas, a marina to rent kayaks and canoes, a 300-foot (91 m) beach and swimming area, seasonal refreshment stand, picnic areas, shelter houses, campsites, cabins, six hiking trials, and ten miles (16 km) of bridal trails. Scuba diving and sailing are also popular activities since no motorized boats are allowed on the lake.

CHECK IN:

CHECK OUT:

PARK HOURS:

DISTANCE:

FEE(S):..

WILL I RETURN?   ❑ YES   ❑ NO

LODGING:

SIGHTS

WHO I WENT WITH

ACTIVITIES

❑ ATV/OHV	❑ Horseback Riding	❑ Wildlife
❑ Berry Picking	❑ Kayaking	❑ Bird Viewing
❑ Biking	❑ Photography	❑ ....
❑ Boating	❑ Skiing	❑ ....
❑ Canoeing	❑ Skijoring	❑ ....
❑ Fishing	❑ Snowshoeing	❑ ....
❑ Hiking	❑ Snowmobiling	❑ ....
❑ Hunting	❑ Swimming	❑ ....

FACILITIES

❑ ADA	❑ Visitor Center	❑	❑ ....
❑ Gift Shop	❑ Picnic Sites	❑	❑ ....
❑ Museum	❑ Restrooms	❑	❑ ....

Rating

⭐ ⭐ ⭐ ⭐ ⭐

Notes

....
....
....
....
....
....
....

PASSPORT STAMPS

LAKE ALMA STATE PARK

Vinton

DATE(S) VISITED:..

❑ SPRING   ❑ SUMMER   ❑ FALL   ❑ WINTER

WEATHER	TEMP:

❑   ❑   ❑   ❑   ❑   ❑

Address

422 Lake Alma Road,
Wellston, Ohio   45692

About this State Park

In the midst of some of Ohio's most rugged, scenic territory lies
Lake Alma State Park. A quiet lake and a gentle creek
meandering through a wooded valley provide a restful setting
for park visitors.
Lake Alma offers 60 campsites suitable for tents or trailers. All
sites are wooded and have electricity. Pet camping is available
on designated sites. Facilities include pit latrines, tables, fire
rings, dump station and drinking water.

CHECK IN:

CHECK OUT:

PARK HOURS:

DISTANCE:

FEE(S):..

WILL I RETURN?   ❑ YES   ❑ NO

LODGING:

WHO I WENT WITH

SIGHTS

ACTIVITIES

- ❏ ATV/OHV
- ❏ Berry Picking
- ❏ Biking
- ❏ Boating
- ❏ Canoeing
- ❏ Fishing
- ❏ Hiking
- ❏ Hunting

- ❏ Horseback Riding
- ❏ Kayaking
- ❏ Photography
- ❏ Skiing
- ❏ Skijoring
- ❏ Snowshoeing
- ❏ Snowmobiling
- ❏ Swimming

- ❏ Wildlife
- ❏ Bird Viewing
- ❏ ....
- ❏ ....
- ❏ ....
- ❏ ....
- ❏ ....
- ❏ ....

FACILITIES

- ❏ ADA
- ❏ Gift Shop
- ❏ Museum

- ❏ Visitor Center
- ❏ Picnic Sites
- ❏ Restrooms

- ❏ ....
- ❏ ....
- ❏ ....

- ❏ ....
- ❏ ....
- ❏ ....

Rating

★ ★ ★ ★ ★

Notes

....
....
....
....
....
....
....
....

PASSPORT STAMPS

LAKE HOPE STATE PARK

Vinton

DATE(S) VISITED: ....

❑ SPRING   ❑ SUMMER   ❑ FALL   ❑ WINTER

WEATHER	TEMP:

❑   ❑   ❑   ❑   ❑   ❑

Address

27331 OH-278,
McArthur, Ohio
45651

About this State Park

Lake Hope State Park is a public recreation area encompassing 2,983 acres (1,207 ha) within Zaleski State Forest, located five miles (8.0 km) northeast of Zaleski in Vinton County, Ohio. The state park is centered on Lake Hope, a 120-acre (49 ha) impoundment on Big Sandy Run.
The park features boating, fishing, swimming, hiking and mountain biking trails, lodge, cottages, and campground.

CHECK IN:

CHECK OUT:

PARK HOURS:

DISTANCE:

FEE(S): ....

WILL I RETURN?   ❑ YES   ❑ NO

LODGING:

WHO I WENT WITH

SIGHTS

ACTIVITIES

- ❑ ATV/OHV
- ❑ Berry Picking
- ❑ Biking
- ❑ Boating
- ❑ Canoeing
- ❑ Fishing
- ❑ Hiking
- ❑ Hunting

- ❑ Horseback Riding
- ❑ Kayaking
- ❑ Photography
- ❑ Skiing
- ❑ Skijoring
- ❑ Snowshoeing
- ❑ Snowmobiling
- ❑ Swimming

- ❑ Wildlife
- ❑ Bird Viewing
- ❑ ....
- ❑ ....
- ❑ ....
- ❑ ....
- ❑ ....
- ❑ ....

FACILITIES

- ❑ ADA
- ❑ Gift Shop
- ❑ Museum

- ❑ Visitor Center
- ❑ Picnic Sites
- ❑ Restrooms

- ❑ ....
- ❑ ....
- ❑ ....

- ❑ ....
- ❑ ....
- ❑ ....

Rating

⭐ ⭐ ⭐ ⭐ ⭐

Notes

....
....
....
....
....
....
....
....

PASSPORT STAMPS

LAKE LOGAN STATE PARK

Hocking

DATE(S) VISITED:...

❑ SPRING ❑ SUMMER ❑ FALL ❑ WINTER

Address

20160 St. Rt. 664,
Logan, Ohio 43138

WEATHER			TEMP:		
❑	❑	❑	❑	❑	❑

About this State Park

Lake Logan State Park is an Ohio state park in Hocking County. Lake Logan State Park is located in Falls Township, Hocking County, Ohio. Lake Logan Dam is directly accessible off State Route 664 just southwest of the county seat of Logan. Lake Logan State Park lies in the Hocking Valley, formed by the Hocking River. Lake Logan was created in 1955 with the construction of the Lake Logan Dam on Clear Fork Creek, a tributary of the Hocking River. Lake Logan is a 400-acre (160 ha) lake and is open to fishing, boating, ice fishing, ice boating and swimming.

CHECK IN:

CHECK OUT:

PARK HOURS:

DISTANCE:

FEE(S):...

WILL I RETURN? ❑ YES ❑ NO

LODGING:

SIGHTS

WHO I WENT WITH

ACTIVITIES

❑ ATV/OHV	❑ Horseback Riding	❑ Wildlife
❑ Berry Picking	❑ Kayaking	❑ Bird Viewing
❑ Biking	❑ Photography	❑ ....
❑ Boating	❑ Skiing	❑ ....
❑ Canoeing	❑ Skijoring	❑ ....
❑ Fishing	❑ Snowshoeing	❑ ....
❑ Hiking	❑ Snowmobiling	❑ ....
❑ Hunting	❑ Swimming	❑ ....

FACILITIES

❑ ADA	❑ Visitor Center	❑	❑ ....
❑ Gift Shop	❑ Picnic Sites	❑	❑ ....
❑ Museum	❑ Restrooms	❑	❑ ....

Rating

⭐ ⭐ ⭐ ⭐ ⭐

Notes

....

....

....

....

....

....

....

....

PASSPORT STAMPS

LAKE LORAMIE STATE PARK

Auglaize

DATE(S) VISITED:..

❑ SPRING   ❑ SUMMER   ❑ FALL   ❑ WINTER

WEATHER			TEMP:		
❑	❑	❑	❑	❑	❑

Address

4401 Fort Loramie-
Swanders Rd
Minster, Ohio   45865

About this State Park

Lake Loramie State Park is a public recreation area located on
the northeast side of Fort Loramie, Ohio. It occupies 407 acres
(165 ha) on 1,655-acre (670 ha) Lake Loramie[3] and is operated
by the Ohio Department of Natural Resources.
One of the original canal feeder lakes, Lake Loramie State Park
offers visitors a quiet retreat in rural Ohio. Swim from the
sandy beach, hike along the old canal towpath, stay a night in a
shaded campsite or boat the lazy waters of Lake Loramie.

CHECK IN:

CHECK OUT:

PARK HOURS:

DISTANCE:

FEE(S):..

WILL I RETURN?   ❑ YES   ❑ NO

LODGING:

SIGHTS

WHO I WENT WITH

ACTIVITIES

- ❑ ATV/OHV
- ❑ Berry Picking
- ❑ Biking
- ❑ Boating
- ❑ Canoeing
- ❑ Fishing
- ❑ Hiking
- ❑ Hunting

- ❑ Horseback Riding
- ❑ Kayaking
- ❑ Photography
- ❑ Skiing
- ❑ Skijoring
- ❑ Snowshoeing
- ❑ Snowmobiling
- ❑ Swimming

- ❑ Wildlife
- ❑ Bird Viewing
- ❑ ....
- ❑ ....
- ❑ ....
- ❑ ....
- ❑ ....
- ❑ ....

FACILITIES

- ❑ ADA
- ❑ Gift Shop
- ❑ Museum

- ❑ Visitor Center
- ❑ Picnic Sites
- ❑ Restrooms

- ❑ ....
- ❑ ....
- ❑ ....

- ❑ ....
- ❑ ....
- ❑ ....

Rating

★ ★ ★ ★ ★

Notes

....

....

....

....

....

....

....

....

PASSPORT STAMPS

LAKE WHITE STATE PARK

Pike

DATE(S) VISITED:..

❑ SPRING ❑ SUMMER ❑ FALL ❑ WINTER

WEATHER				TEMP:	
❑	❑	❑	❑	❑	❑

Address

2767 OH-551
Waverly, Ohio   45690

About this State Park

Lake White State Park is a public recreation area located on the southwest edge of Waverly in Pike County. The state park contains 92 acres (37 ha) of land and 337 acres (136 ha) of water.
Picturesque Lake White is nestled between the ridges of southern Ohio's rugged hills. Water sports enthusiasts can enjoy swimming, boating, water skiing and fishing at this scenic park.

CHECK IN:

CHECK OUT:

PARK HOURS:

DISTANCE:

FEE(S):..

WILL I RETURN? ❑ YES ❑ NO

LODGING:

SIGHTS

WHO I WENT WITH

ACTIVITIES

- ❏ ATV/OHV
- ❏ Berry Picking
- ❏ Biking
- ❏ Boating
- ❏ Canoeing
- ❏ Fishing
- ❏ Hiking
- ❏ Hunting

- ❏ Horseback Riding
- ❏ Kayaking
- ❏ Photography
- ❏ Skiing
- ❏ Skijoring
- ❏ Snowshoeing
- ❏ Snowmobiling
- ❏ Swimming

- ❏ Wildlife
- ❏ Bird Viewing
- ❏ ....
- ❏ ....
- ❏ ....
- ❏ ....
- ❏ ....
- ❏ ....

FACILITIES

- ❏ ADA
- ❏ Gift Shop
- ❏ Museum

- ❏ Visitor Center
- ❏ Picnic Sites
- ❏ Restrooms

- ❏ ....
- ❏ ....
- ❏ ....

- ❏ ....
- ❏ ....
- ❏ ....

Rating

⭐ ⭐ ⭐ ⭐ ⭐

Notes

....
....
....
....
....
....
....
....

PASSPORT STAMPS

LITTLE MIAMI STATE PARK

Hamilton, Clermont,
Warren, Greene

DATE(S) VISITED:..

❑ SPRING   ❑ SUMMER   ❑ FALL   ❑ WINTER

WEATHER	TEMP:
☀ ❄☁ ☁ ☁ 🌧 ☁🌧 ☁🌧	
❑ ❑ ❑ ❑ ❑ ❑	

Address

8570 East State Route
73 Waynesville,
Ohio 45068

About this State Park

The Little Miami Scenic Trail is the fourth longest paved trail in the United States, running 78.1 miles (125.7 km) through five southwestern counties in the state of Ohio. The multi-use rail trail sees heavy recreational use by hikers and bicyclists, as well as the occasional horseback rider.

Most of the trail runs along the banks of the Little Miami River, in a dedicated, car-free corridor known as Little Miami State Park. This unusually linear state park passes through four counties, with a right-of-way running about 50 miles (80 km) long and averaging 66 feet (20 m) in width for a total of about 400 acres (160 ha). Elsewhere, the corridor ranges from 8 to 10 feet (2.4 to 3.0 m) in width.

CHECK IN:

CHECK OUT:

PARK HOURS:

DISTANCE:

FEE(S):...

WILL I RETURN?   ❑ YES   ❑ NO

LODGING:

SIGHTS

WHO I WENT WITH

ACTIVITIES

- ❑ ATV/OHV
- ❑ Berry Picking
- ❑ Biking
- ❑ Boating
- ❑ Canoeing
- ❑ Fishing
- ❑ Hiking
- ❑ Hunting

- ❑ Horseback Riding
- ❑ Kayaking
- ❑ Photography
- ❑ Skiing
- ❑ Skijoring
- ❑ Snowshoeing
- ❑ Snowmobiling
- ❑ Swimming

- ❑ Wildlife
- ❑ Bird Viewing
- ❑ ....
- ❑ ....
- ❑ ....
- ❑ ....
- ❑ ....
- ❑ ....

FACILITIES

- ❑ ADA
- ❑ Gift Shop
- ❑ Museum

- ❑ Visitor Center
- ❑ Picnic Sites
- ❑ Restrooms

- ❑ ....
- ❑ ....
- ❑ ....

- ❑ ....
- ❑ ....
- ❑ ....

Rating

★ ★ ★ ★ ★

Notes

....
....
....
....
....
....
....

| PASSPORT STAMPS |

MADISON LAKE STATE PARK

Madison

DATE(S) VISITED:..

❏ SPRING   ❏ SUMMER   ❏ FALL   ❏ WINTER

WEATHER			TEMP:		
☀	❄☁	☁	☁	☁	☁
❏	❏	❏	❏	❏	❏

Address

4860 E Park Dr
London, Ohio   43140

About this State Park

Madison Lake State Park is a public recreation area located four miles (6.4 km) east of London in the Darby Plains region of Madison County. The state park includes 106-acre (43 ha) Madison Lake and 76 acres (31 ha) of surrounding land.
The park offers a boat ramp, 300-foot (91 m) sand beach, changing booths and restrooms, picnic areas, and shelters. A mile-long hiking trial skirts the lake's southern shore. The lake's northern end is reserved for hunting migratory game birds. The park is a popular fishing location, with bass, bluegill, crappie, and channel catfish found in the lake.

CHECK IN:

CHECK OUT:

PARK HOURS:

DISTANCE:

FEE(S):..

WILL I RETURN?   ❏ YES   ❏ NO

LODGING:

SIGHTS

WHO I WENT WITH

ACTIVITIES

❑ ATV/OHV	❑ Horseback Riding	❑ Wildlife
❑ Berry Picking	❑ Kayaking	❑ Bird Viewing
❑ Biking	❑ Photography	❑ ....
❑ Boating	❑ Skiing	❑ ....
❑ Canoeing	❑ Skijoring	❑ ....
❑ Fishing	❑ Snowshoeing	❑ ....
❑ Hiking	❑ Snowmobiling	❑ ....
❑ Hunting	❑ Swimming	❑ ....

FACILITIES

❑ ADA	❑ Visitor Center	❑	❑ ....
❑ Gift Shop	❑ Picnic Sites	❑	❑ ....
❑ Museum	❑ Restrooms	❑	❑ ....

Rating

⭐ ⭐ ⭐ ⭐ ⭐

Notes

....
....
....
....
....
....
....
....

PASSPORT STAMPS

MALABAR FARM STATE PARK

Richland

DATE(S) VISITED:...

❑ SPRING   ❑ SUMMER   ❑ FALL   ❑ WINTER

WEATHER		TEMP:	
❑	❑	❑	❑ ❑ ❑

Address

4050 Bromfield Rd
Lucas, Ohio 44843-9745

About this State Park

Malabar Farm in Pleasant Valley was the dream of the Pulitzer Prize-winning author, Louis Bromfield. Today, visitors can see the house and farm existing just as they did in Bromfield's time. The outbuildings and pastures still house chickens, goats and beef cattle. The hills are ribboned with strips of corn, wheat, oats and hay while the scenic trails are adorned with nature's bounty.
A fifteen-site horseman's camp offers primitive camping for horsepeople as well as family campers. Fire rings, picnic tables, drinking water and latrines are offered.

CHECK IN:

CHECK OUT:

PARK HOURS:

DISTANCE:

FEE(S):..

WILL I RETURN?   ❑ YES   ❑ NO

LODGING:

SIGHTS

WHO I WENT WITH

ACTIVITIES

❏ ATV/OHV	❏ Horseback Riding	❏ Wildlife
❏ Berry Picking	❏ Kayaking	❏ Bird Viewing
❏ Biking	❏ Photography	❏ ....
❏ Boating	❏ Skiing	❏ ....
❏ Canoeing	❏ Skijoring	❏ ....
❏ Fishing	❏ Snowshoeing	❏ ....
❏ Hiking	❏ Snowmobiling	❏ ....
❏ Hunting	❏ Swimming	❏ ....

FACILITIES

❏ ADA	❏ Visitor Center	❏	❏ ....
❏ Gift Shop	❏ Picnic Sites	❏	❏ ....
❏ Museum	❏ Restrooms	❏	❏ ....

Rating

★ ★ ★ ★ ★

Notes

....
....
....
....
....
....
....

PASSPORT STAMPS

MARY JANE THURSTON STATE PARK

Henry

DATE(S) VISITED:..

❏ SPRING   ❏ SUMMER   ❏ FALL   ❏ WINTER

Address

1466 State Rte 65
McClure, Ohio   43534

WEATHER			TEMP:		
❏	❏	❏	❏	❏	❏

About this State Park

Mary Jane Thurston State Park is a 105-acre (42 ha) public recreation area one mile west of Grand Rapids in Wood and Henry counties. The state park lies along the south bank of the Maumee River near remains of the historic Miami and Erie Canal. It is named for Mary Jane Thurston, a schoolteacher from Grand Rapids who bequeathed land for the establishment of a park. The park's year-round recreation includes hunting, fishing, boating, picnicking, and camping.

The park offers camping, boating on the Maumee River, picnicking, hunting, and fishing. Common game animals include white-tailed deer and wild turkeys. The river is home to northern pike, bullhead catfish, smallmouth bass, and crappie. A one-mile stretch of the Buckeye Trail passes through the park.

CHECK IN:

CHECK OUT:

PARK HOURS:

DISTANCE:

FEE(S):..

WILL I RETURN?   ❏ YES   ❏ NO

LODGING:

SIGHTS

WHO I WENT WITH

ACTIVITIES

- ❑ ATV/OHV
- ❑ Berry Picking
- ❑ Biking
- ❑ Boating
- ❑ Canoeing
- ❑ Fishing
- ❑ Hiking
- ❑ Hunting

- ❑ Horseback Riding
- ❑ Kayaking
- ❑ Photography
- ❑ Skiing
- ❑ Skijoring
- ❑ Snowshoeing
- ❑ Snowmobiling
- ❑ Swimming

- ❑ Wildlife
- ❑ Bird Viewing
- ❑ ....
- ❑ ....
- ❑ ....
- ❑ ....
- ❑ ....
- ❑ ....

FACILITIES

- ❑ ADA
- ❑ Gift Shop
- ❑ Museum

- ❑ Visitor Center
- ❑ Picnic Sites
- ❑ Restrooms

- ❑ ....
- ❑ ....
- ❑ ....

- ❑ ....
- ❑ ....
- ❑ ....

Rating

⭐ ⭐ ⭐ ⭐ ⭐

Notes

....
....
....
....
....
....
....
....

PASSPORT STAMPS

MAUMEE BAY STATE PARK

Lucas

DATE(S) VISITED:...

❏ SPRING   ❏ SUMMER   ❏ FALL   ❏ WINTER

WEATHER		TEMP:			
❏	❏	❏	❏	❏	❏

Address

1400 State Park Road
Oregon, Ohio   43616

About this State Park

Maumee Bay State Park is a 1,336-acre (541 ha) public recreation area located on the shores of Lake Erie, five miles east of Toledo, in Jerusalem Township, Lucas County. Major features of the state park include a lodge and conference center, cottages, camping facilities, golf course, nature center, and two-mile-long interpretive boardwalk. Common activities include hiking, picnicking, fishing, hunting, boating, swimming, winter sports, and geocaching. The site was acquired by the state in 1974 and became a state park in 1975.

Maumee Bay State Park offers not only the finest of recreational facilities in the Midwest, but also a unique natural environment created by the convergence of the land and Lake Erie. The lodge, cottages and golf course are nestled among the scenic meadows, wet woods and lush marshes teeming with wildlife. The balance of recreational facilities with the natural world gives visitors a diverse experience in a coastal environment.

CHECK IN:

CHECK OUT:

PARK HOURS:

DISTANCE:

FEE(S):...

WILL I RETURN?   ❏ YES   ❏ NO

LODGING:

SIGHTS

WHO I WENT WITH

ACTIVITIES

- ❏ ATV/OHV
- ❏ Berry Picking
- ❏ Biking
- ❏ Boating
- ❏ Canoeing
- ❏ Fishing
- ❏ Hiking
- ❏ Hunting

- ❏ Horseback Riding
- ❏ Kayaking
- ❏ Photography
- ❏ Skiing
- ❏ Skijoring
- ❏ Snowshoeing
- ❏ Snowmobiling
- ❏ Swimming

- ❏ Wildlife
- ❏ Bird Viewing
- ❏ ....
- ❏ ....
- ❏ ....
- ❏ ....
- ❏ ....
- ❏ ....

FACILITIES

- ❏ ADA
- ❏ Gift Shop
- ❏ Museum

- ❏ Visitor Center
- ❏ Picnic Sites
- ❏ Restrooms

- ❏ ....
- ❏ ....
- ❏ ....

- ❏ ....
- ❏ ....
- ❏ ....

Rating

★ ★ ★ ★ ★

Notes

....
....
....
....
....
....
....
....

PASSPORT STAMPS

MOHICAN STATE PARK

Ashland, Holmes

DATE(S) VISITED:..

❑ SPRING   ❑ SUMMER   ❑ FALL   ❑ WINTER

WEATHER		TEMP:			
☀	❄☁	☁	☁🌧	☁🌧	☁
❑	❑	❑	❑	❑	❑

Address

3116 OH-3
Loudonville,
Ohio 44842

About this State Park

Mohican State Park is a 1,110-acre (450 ha) public recreation area located on the south shore of Pleasant Hill Lake, five miles (8.0 km) south of Loudonville in Ashland County. The state park is located along Ohio SR 3 and Ohio SR 97 and is surrounded by the 4,525-acre (1,831 ha) Mohican-Memorial State Forest. The Clear Fork of the Mohican River flows through the park carving a narrow gorge and joins the Black Fork about a half-mile east of the park to form the Mohican River. The park is open for year-round recreation including camping, hiking, boating, mountain biking, fishing, and picnicking.

Mohican State Park and the adjacent state forest are outstanding in their beauty and offer limitless opportunities for visitors to explore one of Ohio's most unique natural regions. The striking Clearfork Gorge, hemlock forest and scenic Mohican River offer a wilderness experience while the resort lodge and cottages provide luxurious accommodations.

CHECK IN:

CHECK OUT:

PARK HOURS:

DISTANCE:

FEE(S):..

WILL I RETURN?   ❑ YES   ❑ NO

LODGING:

SIGHTS

WHO I WENT WITH

ACTIVITIES

❑ ATV/OHV	❑ Horseback Riding	❑ Wildlife
❑ Berry Picking	❑ Kayaking	❑ Bird Viewing
❑ Biking	❑ Photography	❑ ....
❑ Boating	❑ Skiing	❑ ....
❑ Canoeing	❑ Skijoring	❑ ....
❑ Fishing	❑ Snowshoeing	❑ ....
❑ Hiking	❑ Snowmobiling	❑ ....
❑ Hunting	❑ Swimming	❑ ....

FACILITIES

❑ ADA	❑ Visitor Center	❑	❑ ....
❑ Gift Shop	❑ Picnic Sites	❑	❑ ....
❑ Museum	❑ Restrooms	❑	❑ ....

Rating

★ ★ ★ ★ ★

Notes

....
....
....
....
....
....
....

PASSPORT STAMPS

MOSQUITO LAKE STATE PARK

Trumbull

DATE(S) VISITED:...

❑ SPRING   ❑ SUMMER   ❑ FALL   ❑ WINTER

WEATHER			TEMP:		
❑	❑	❑	❑	❑	❑

About this State Park

Mosquito Creek Lake is a man-made reservoir. It is the second-largest inland lake in Ohio. Depth averages 8 to 15 feet (2.4 to 4.6 m) (depending on season), but the southern end towards the dam averages 20 to 25 feet (6.1 to 7.6 m). The northern end is considerably more shallow, with depths averaging only 4 to 10 feet (1.2 to 3.0 m). Completely surrounding the lake is Mosquito Lake State Park, and it is bisected by the Ohio State Route 88 causeway. The drainage area for lake is 97.4 square miles (252 km2).

The lake is surrounded by Mosquito Lake State Park, operated by the Ohio Department of Natural Resources. There are picnicking and camping, as well as designated hiking trails. Opportunities for water recreation are provided, including dock rentals, boat ramps, and various watercraft rentals. Fishing for flathead catfish is highly recommended at the location. Other species recreationally fished in the lake are bluegill, channel catfish, crappie, largemouth bass, northern pike, ring perch, and walleye.

CHECK IN:

CHECK OUT:

PARK HOURS:

DISTANCE:

FEE(S):...

WILL I RETURN?   ❑ YES   ❑ NO

LODGING:

SIGHTS

WHO I WENT WITH

ACTIVITIES

❑ ATV/OHV	❑ Horseback Riding	❑ Wildlife
❑ Berry Picking	❑ Kayaking	❑ Bird Viewing
❑ Biking	❑ Photography	❑ ....
❑ Boating	❑ Skiing	❑ ....
❑ Canoeing	❑ Skijoring	❑ ....
❑ Fishing	❑ Snowshoeing	❑ ....
❑ Hiking	❑ Snowmobiling	❑ ....
❑ Hunting	❑ Swimming	❑ ....

FACILITIES

❑ ADA	❑ Visitor Center	❑	❑ ....
❑ Gift Shop	❑ Picnic Sites	❑	❑ ....
❑ Museum	❑ Restrooms	❑	❑ ....

Rating

★ ★ ★ ★ ★

Notes

....
....
....
....
....
....
....
....

PASSPORT STAMPS

MOUNT GILEAD STATE PARK

Morrow

DATE(S) VISITED:..

❏ SPRING   ❏ SUMMER   ❏ FALL   ❏ WINTER

WEATHER	TEMP:
❏ ❏ ❏ ❏ ❏ ❏	

Address

4119 OH-95
Mt Gilead,
Ohio   43338

About this State Park

Mt. Gilead State Park is a public recreation area located immediately to the east of the village of Mount Gilead in Morrow County. The state park covers 181 acres (73 ha), 32 of which are the upper and lower lakes. It offers hiking, camping, picnicking, fishing and electric-motor boating as well as wintertime ice skating, ice fishing, and cross-country skiing. Access to the park is via State Route 95.

CHECK IN:

CHECK OUT:

PARK HOURS:

DISTANCE:

FEE(S):..

WILL I RETURN?   ❏ YES   ❏ NO

LODGING:

SIGHTS

WHO I WENT WITH

ACTIVITIES

❏ ATV/OHV	❏ Horseback Riding	❏ Wildlife
❏ Berry Picking	❏ Kayaking	❏ Bird Viewing
❏ Biking	❏ Photography	❏ ....
❏ Boating	❏ Skiing	❏ ....
❏ Canoeing	❏ Skijoring	❏ ....
❏ Fishing	❏ Snowshoeing	❏ ....
❏ Hiking	❏ Snowmobiling	❏ ....
❏ Hunting	❏ Swimming	❏ ....

FACILITIES

❏ ADA	❏ Visitor Center	❏	❏ ....
❏ Gift Shop	❏ Picnic Sites	❏	❏ ....
❏ Museum	❏ Restrooms	❏	❏ ....

Rating

★ ★ ★ ★ ★

Notes

....
....
....
....
....
....
....
....

PASSPORT STAMPS

NELSON KENNEDY LEDGES STATE PARK

Portage

DATE(S) VISITED:...

❑ SPRING   ❑ SUMMER   ❑ FALL   ❑ WINTER

WEATHER			TEMP:		
☀	❄☁	☁	🌧	⛈	🌨
❑	❑	❑	❑	❑	❑

Address

12440 OH-282
Garrettsville,
Ohio 44231

About this State Park

Nelson-Kennedy Ledges State Park is a 167-acre (68 ha) public recreation area offering trails and picnicking located in Nelson Township, Portage County. Within the park are angled rock formations 50 to 60 feet (18 m) high with ground fissures as deep as 60 feet (18 m). It is accessible from U.S. Route 422 and State Route 305 via State Route 282.

The park is open from dawn until dusk. There are approximately 3 miles (4.8 km) of main hiking trails, as well as many unmarked and more dangerous paths. To mark off the trails, a color-coding system is used on the rocks and trees. White is moderately easy, yellow and blue are medium difficulty, and red is extremely difficult, with some climbing of rocks involved.

Because of the cliffs and hazards along the trails, night hiking is not recommended due to the decreased visibility.

CHECK IN:

CHECK OUT:

PARK HOURS:

DISTANCE:

FEE(S):...

WILL I RETURN?   ❑ YES   ❑ NO

LODGING:

SIGHTS

WHO I WENT WITH

ACTIVITIES

- ❏ ATV/OHV
- ❏ Berry Picking
- ❏ Biking
- ❏ Boating
- ❏ Canoeing
- ❏ Fishing
- ❏ Hiking
- ❏ Hunting

- ❏ Horseback Riding
- ❏ Kayaking
- ❏ Photography
- ❏ Skiing
- ❏ Skijoring
- ❏ Snowshoeing
- ❏ Snowmobiling
- ❏ Swimming

- ❏ Wildlife
- ❏ Bird Viewing
- ❏ ....
- ❏ ....
- ❏ ....
- ❏ ....
- ❏ ....

FACILITIES

- ❏ ADA
- ❏ Gift Shop
- ❏ Museum

- ❏ Visitor Center
- ❏ Picnic Sites
- ❏ Restrooms

- ❏ ....
- ❏ ....
- ❏ ....

- ❏ ....
- ❏ ....
- ❏ ....

Rating

★ ★ ★ ★ ★

Notes

....
....
....
....
....
....
....
....

PASSPORT STAMPS

OAK POINT STATE PARK

Ottawa

DATE(S) VISITED:..

❑ SPRING   ❑ SUMMER   ❑ FALL   ❑ WINTER

WEATHER	TEMP:
❑ ❑ ❑ ❑ ❑ ❑	

About this State Park

Oak Point State Park is the smallest park in Ohio's state park system. Clocking in at 1.5 acres, this little oasis is a lovely spot to visit while on Put-in-Bay. Despite its size, it offers a range of facilities for boaters and picnickers alike. Come down and enjoy the panoramic views of Put-in-Bay and beautiful Lake Erie. This is also a spectacular place to watch the sunrise, if you can get up that early!
Twenty docks are available for either daily or overnight rentals. Whenever you are boating on Lake Erie, it is imperative to follow the Ohio Boating Laws to make sure everyone in your boat and others are safe. The docks are accessed via a U-shaped driveway.

CHECK IN:

CHECK OUT:

PARK HOURS:

DISTANCE:

FEE(S):..

WILL I RETURN?   ❑ YES   ❑ NO

LODGING:

SIGHTS

WHO I WENT WITH

ACTIVITIES

- ❑ ATV/OHV
- ❑ Berry Picking
- ❑ Biking
- ❑ Boating
- ❑ Canoeing
- ❑ Fishing
- ❑ Hiking
- ❑ Hunting

- ❑ Horseback Riding
- ❑ Kayaking
- ❑ Photography
- ❑ Skiing
- ❑ Skijoring
- ❑ Snowshoeing
- ❑ Snowmobiling
- ❑ Swimming

- ❑ Wildlife
- ❑ Bird Viewing
- ❑ ....
- ❑ ....
- ❑ ....
- ❑ ....
- ❑ ....
- ❑ ....

FACILITIES

- ❑ ADA
- ❑ Gift Shop
- ❑ Museum

- ❑ Visitor Center
- ❑ Picnic Sites
- ❑ Restrooms

- ❑ ....
- ❑ ....
- ❑ ....

- ❑ ....
- ❑ ....
- ❑ ....

Rating

⭐ ⭐ ⭐ ⭐ ⭐

Notes

....
....
....
....
....
....
....
....

PASSPORT STAMPS

PAINT CREEK STATE PARK

Ross

DATE(S) VISITED:...

❑ SPRING   ❑ SUMMER   ❑ FALL   ❑ WINTER

WEATHER			TEMP:		
❑	❑	❑	❑	❑	❑

Address

280 Taylor Rd
Bainbridge,
Ohio   45612

About this State Park

Located amid the breathtaking scenery of the Paint Creek Valley, Paint Creek State Park features a large lake with fine fishing, boating and swimming opportunities. A modern campground and meandering trails invite outdoor enthusiasts to explore and enjoy the rolling hills and streams of this scenic area.

The state park's central feature is a reservoir, 1,148-acre (465 ha) Paint Creek Lake, which was created by the damming of Paint Creek. Construction on the dam started in 1967, and Paint Creek State Park was opened in 1972.

CHECK IN:

CHECK OUT:

PARK HOURS:

DISTANCE:

FEE(S):..

WILL I RETURN?   ❑ YES   ❑ NO

LODGING:

SIGHTS

WHO I WENT WITH

ACTIVITIES

- ❑ ATV/OHV
- ❑ Berry Picking
- ❑ Biking
- ❑ Boating
- ❑ Canoeing
- ❑ Fishing
- ❑ Hiking
- ❑ Hunting

- ❑ Horseback Riding
- ❑ Kayaking
- ❑ Photography
- ❑ Skiing
- ❑ Skijoring
- ❑ Snowshoeing
- ❑ Snowmobiling
- ❑ Swimming

- ❑ Wildlife
- ❑ Bird Viewing
- ❑ ....
- ❑ ....
- ❑ ....
- ❑ ....
- ❑ ....
- ❑ ....

FACILITIES

- ❑ ADA
- ❑ Gift Shop
- ❑ Museum

- ❑ Visitor Center
- ❑ Picnic Sites
- ❑ Restrooms

- ❑ ....
- ❑ ....
- ❑ ....

- ❑ ....
- ❑ ....
- ❑ ....

Rating

★ ★ ★ ★ ★

Notes

....
....
....
....
....
....
....
....

PASSPORT STAMPS

PIKE LAKE STATE PARK

Ross

DATE(S) VISITED:..

❏ SPRING ❏ SUMMER ❏ FALL ❏ WINTER

WEATHER		TEMP:
❏	❏	❏	❏	❏	❏

Address

1847 Pike Lake Rd
Bainbridge,
Ohio 45612

About this State Park

Pike Lake State Park is a public recreation area located in the midst of the wooded hills of Pike County, five miles south of the village of Bainbridge, in the southern part of the U.S. state of Ohio. The state park contains a small lake with surrounding state forest, campground, and cabins. The site was developed by members of the Civilian Conservation Corps in the 1930s and became a state park in 1949.

CHECK IN:

CHECK OUT:

PARK HOURS:

DISTANCE:

FEE(S):..

WILL I RETURN? ❏ YES ❏ NO

LODGING:

SIGHTS

WHO I WENT WITH

ACTIVITIES

❏ ATV/OHV	❏ Horseback Riding	❏ Wildlife
❏ Berry Picking	❏ Kayaking	❏ Bird Viewing
❏ Biking	❏ Photography	❏ ....
❏ Boating	❏ Skiing	❏ ....
❏ Canoeing	❏ Skijoring	❏ ....
❏ Fishing	❏ Snowshoeing	❏ ....
❏ Hiking	❏ Snowmobiling	❏ ....
❏ Hunting	❏ Swimming	❏ ....

FACILITIES

❏ ADA	❏ Visitor Center	❏	❏ ....
❏ Gift Shop	❏ Picnic Sites	❏	❏ ....
❏ Museum	❏ Restrooms	❏	❏ ....

Rating

⭐ ⭐ ⭐ ⭐ ⭐

Notes

....

....

....

....

....

....

....

PASSPORT STAMPS

PORTAGE LAKES STATE PARK

Summit

DATE(S) VISITED:..

❑ SPRING   ❑ SUMMER   ❑ FALL   ❑ WINTER

WEATHER				TEMP:	
☀ ❄☁	☁	☁	☁	☁	☁
❑	❑	❑	❑	❑	❑

Address

5031 Manchester Rd
Akron, Ohio   44319

About this State Park

Portage Lakes State Park is a public recreation area located around the Portage Lakes in New Franklin. The eight Portage Lakes encompass 2,034 acres (823 ha) used for boating, fishing, and swimming. The Ohio Department of Public Works turned over maintenance of the lakes to the Ohio Department of Natural Resources Division of Parks and Recreation in 1949. The wetlands of the park attract waterfowl and shorebirds providing visitors enjoyment whether hunting or observing wildlife.

CHECK IN:

CHECK OUT:

PARK HOURS:

DISTANCE:

FEE(S):..

WILL I RETURN?   ❑ YES   ❑ NO

LODGING:

SIGHTS

WHO I WENT WITH

ACTIVITIES

- ❑ ATV/OHV
- ❑ Berry Picking
- ❑ Biking
- ❑ Boating
- ❑ Canoeing
- ❑ Fishing
- ❑ Hiking
- ❑ Hunting

- ❑ Horseback Riding
- ❑ Kayaking
- ❑ Photography
- ❑ Skiing
- ❑ Skijoring
- ❑ Snowshoeing
- ❑ Snowmobiling
- ❑ Swimming

- ❑ Wildlife
- ❑ Bird Viewing
- ❑ ....
- ❑ ....
- ❑ ....
- ❑ ....
- ❑ ....
- ❑ ....

FACILITIES

- ❑ ADA
- ❑ Gift Shop
- ❑ Museum

- ❑ Visitor Center
- ❑ Picnic Sites
- ❑ Restrooms

- ❑ ....
- ❑ ....
- ❑ ....

- ❑ ....
- ❑ ....
- ❑ ....

Rating

⭐ ⭐ ⭐ ⭐ ⭐

Notes

....
....
....
....
....
....
....
....

PASSPORT STAMPS

PUNDERSON STATE PARK

Geauga

DATE(S) VISITED:...

❑ SPRING   ❑ SUMMER   ❑ FALL   ❑ WINTER

WEATHER	TEMP:
❑ ❑ ❑ ❑ ❑ ❑	

Address

11755 Kinsman Rd
Newbury Township,
Ohio   44065

About this State Park

Punderson State Park is a 741-acre (300 ha) public recreation area in Newbury, Ohio. The State Park with its natural lake, resort manor house, family cottages, golf course and scenic campground, provides myriad recreational opportunities for visitors. Punderson is also Ohio's premier winter sports park. Sledding, snowmobiling and cross-country skiing are all at their best.

CHECK IN:

CHECK OUT:

PARK HOURS:

DISTANCE:

FEE(S):...

WILL I RETURN?   ❑ YES   ❑ NO

LODGING:

WHO I WENT WITH

SIGHTS

ACTIVITIES

- ❑ ATV/OHV
- ❑ Berry Picking
- ❑ Biking
- ❑ Boating
- ❑ Canoeing
- ❑ Fishing
- ❑ Hiking
- ❑ Hunting

- ❑ Horseback Riding
- ❑ Kayaking
- ❑ Photography
- ❑ Skiing
- ❑ Skijoring
- ❑ Snowshoeing
- ❑ Snowmobiling
- ❑ Swimming

- ❑ Wildlife
- ❑ Bird Viewing
- ❑ ....
- ❑ ....
- ❑ ....
- ❑ ....
- ❑ ....
- ❑ ....

FACILITIES

- ❑ ADA
- ❑ Gift Shop
- ❑ Museum

- ❑ Visitor Center
- ❑ Picnic Sites
- ❑ Restrooms

- ❑ ....
- ❑ ....
- ❑ ....

- ❑ ....
- ❑ ....
- ❑ ....

Rating

★ ★ ★ ★ ★

Notes

....
....
....
....
....
....
....
....

PASSPORT STAMPS

PYMATUNING STATE PARK

Ashtabula

DATE(S) VISITED:..

❏ SPRING   ❏ SUMMER   ❏ FALL   ❏ WINTER

Address

6100 Pymatuning Lake Rd
Andover, Ohio 44003

WEATHER	TEMP:

❏   ❏   ❏   ❏   ❏   ❏

About this State Park

In a setting that highlights the mystery of an old swamp forest and the excitement of a water recreation area, Pymatuning State Park invites outdoor lovers of all ages to enjoy a relaxing lakeside vacation experience. In addition to being one of the finest walleye and muskellunge lakes in the country, Pymatuning offers excellent camping, swimming and boating opportunities as well.

CHECK IN:

CHECK OUT:

PARK HOURS:

DISTANCE:

FEE(S):...

WILL I RETURN?   ❏ YES   ❏ NO

LODGING:

SIGHTS

WHO I WENT WITH

ACTIVITIES

- ❏ ATV/OHV
- ❏ Berry Picking
- ❏ Biking
- ❏ Boating
- ❏ Canoeing
- ❏ Fishing
- ❏ Hiking
- ❏ Hunting

- ❏ Horseback Riding
- ❏ Kayaking
- ❏ Photography
- ❏ Skiing
- ❏ Skijoring
- ❏ Snowshoeing
- ❏ Snowmobiling
- ❏ Swimming

- ❏ Wildlife
- ❏ Bird Viewing
- ❏ ....
- ❏ ....
- ❏ ....
- ❏ ....
- ❏ ....
- ❏ ....

FACILITIES

- ❏ ADA
- ❏ Gift Shop
- ❏ Museum

- ❏ Visitor Center
- ❏ Picnic Sites
- ❏ Restrooms

- ❏ ....
- ❏ ....
- ❏ ....

- ❏ ....
- ❏ ....
- ❏ ....

Rating

★ ★ ★ ★ ★

Notes

....
....
....
....
....
....
....
....

PASSPORT STAMPS

QUAIL HOLLOW STATE PARK

Stark

DATE(S) VISITED:...

❑ SPRING ❑ SUMMER ❑ FALL ❑ WINTER

WEATHER	TEMP:
❑ ❑ ❑ ❑ ❑ ❑	

Address

13480 Congress Lake Ave NE
Hartville, Ohio 44632

About this State Park

Quail Hollow Park is a 703-acre (284 ha) county park in Stark County. The park was opened to the public in 1975. It was previously a privately owned family farm and later a hunting camp.

Quail Hollow Park is open for year-round recreation. There is a primitive campground that is open to large groups such as the Scouts and church youth groups. The campground is remote and is without running water or trash facilities. All water and trash must be carried in and out. The park has 19 miles of trails open to hiking, mountain biking and cross-country skiing. Careful observers will see some wildlife along the trail along with a variety of plant species. There are eight nature trails in the park. Quail Hollow Park has a five mile horse trail. Shady Lane Pond is open to fishing with a valid Ohio fishing license. The picnic area and playground are near Shady Lane Pond.

CHECK IN:

CHECK OUT:

PARK HOURS:

DISTANCE:

FEE(S):..

WILL I RETURN? ❑ YES ❑ NO

LODGING:

SIGHTS

WHO I WENT WITH

ACTIVITIES

- ❑ ATV/OHV
- ❑ Berry Picking
- ❑ Biking
- ❑ Boating
- ❑ Canoeing
- ❑ Fishing
- ❑ Hiking
- ❑ Hunting

- ❑ Horseback Riding
- ❑ Kayaking
- ❑ Photography
- ❑ Skiing
- ❑ Skijoring
- ❑ Snowshoeing
- ❑ Snowmobiling
- ❑ Swimming

- ❑ Wildlife
- ❑ Bird Viewing
- ❑ ....
- ❑ ....
- ❑ ....
- ❑ ....
- ❑ ....
- ❑ ....

FACILITIES

- ❑ ADA
- ❑ Gift Shop
- ❑ Museum

- ❑ Visitor Center
- ❑ Picnic Sites
- ❑ Restrooms

- ❑ ....
- ❑ ....
- ❑ ....

- ❑ ....
- ❑ ....
- ❑ ....

Rating

★ ★ ★ ★ ★

Notes

....
....
....
....
....
....
....
....

PASSPORT STAMPS

ROCKY FORK STATE PARK

Highland

DATE(S) VISITED:..

❏ SPRING   ❏ SUMMER   ❏ FALL   ❏ WINTER

WEATHER			TEMP:		
❏	❏	❏	❏	❏	❏

Address

9800 N Shore Dr
Hillsboro, Ohio   45133

About this State Park

Rocky Fork State Park is a public recreation area located in Highland County. The state park's central feature is 2,080-acre (840 ha) Rocky Fork Lake and its 31 miles (50 km) of shoreline. The lake was added to the state park system in 1950. The park offers marinas, boat ramps, swimming beaches, picnic areas, hiking trails and nature center. Two significant archaeological sites dating from the Hopewellian period are located in the park, the Rocky Fork Park Group and the Rocky Fork Park Site.

CHECK IN:

CHECK OUT:

PARK HOURS:

DISTANCE:

FEE(S):..

WILL I RETURN?   ❏ YES   ❏ NO

LODGING:

SIGHTS

WHO I WENT WITH

ACTIVITIES

- ❑ ATV/OHV
- ❑ Berry Picking
- ❑ Biking
- ❑ Boating
- ❑ Canoeing
- ❑ Fishing
- ❑ Hiking
- ❑ Hunting

- ❑ Horseback Riding
- ❑ Kayaking
- ❑ Photography
- ❑ Skiing
- ❑ Skijoring
- ❑ Snowshoeing
- ❑ Snowmobiling
- ❑ Swimming

- ❑ Wildlife
- ❑ Bird Viewing
- ❑ ....
- ❑ ....
- ❑ ....
- ❑ ....
- ❑ ....
- ❑ ....

FACILITIES

- ❑ ADA
- ❑ Gift Shop
- ❑ Museum

- ❑ Visitor Center
- ❑ Picnic Sites
- ❑ Restrooms

- ❑ ....
- ❑ ....
- ❑ ....

- ❑ ....
- ❑ ....
- ❑ ....

Rating

⭐ ⭐ ⭐ ⭐ ⭐

Notes

....
....
....
....
....
....
....
....

PASSPORT STAMPS

SALT FORK STATE PARK

Guernsey

DATE(S) VISITED:...

❑ SPRING   ❑ SUMMER   ❑ FALL   ❑ WINTER

WEATHER	TEMP:
❑ ❑ ❑ ❑ ❑ ❑	

Address

14755 Cadiz Rd
Lore City, Ohio   43755

About this State Park

Salt Fork State Park is a public recreation area located six miles (9.7 km) north of Lore City in Guernsey County. It is the largest state park in Ohio, encompassing 17,229 acres (6,972 ha) of land and 2,952 acres (1,195 ha) of water. The grounds include the Kennedy Stone House, which is listed on the National Register of Historic Places. The park is managed by the Ohio Department of Natural Resources Division of Parks and Watercraft. The park features an 18-hole golf course, 2,500-foot swimming beach, two marinas and seven boat launching ramps, fishing for largemouth bass, crappie, bluegill, walleye and muskellunge, hunting, picnicking facilities, trails for hiking, snowmobiling, and equestrian use, miniature golf, nature center, and an archery range.

CHECK IN:

CHECK OUT:

PARK HOURS:

DISTANCE:

FEE(S):..

WILL I RETURN?   ❑ YES   ❑ NO

LODGING:

SIGHTS

WHO I WENT WITH

ACTIVITIES

- ❑ ATV/OHV
- ❑ Berry Picking
- ❑ Biking
- ❑ Boating
- ❑ Canoeing
- ❑ Fishing
- ❑ Hiking
- ❑ Hunting

- ❑ Horseback Riding
- ❑ Kayaking
- ❑ Photography
- ❑ Skiing
- ❑ Skijoring
- ❑ Snowshoeing
- ❑ Snowmobiling
- ❑ Swimming

- ❑ Wildlife
- ❑ Bird Viewing
- ❑ ....
- ❑ ....
- ❑ ....
- ❑ ....
- ❑ ....
- ❑ ....

FACILITIES

- ❑ ADA
- ❑ Gift Shop
- ❑ Museum

- ❑ Visitor Center
- ❑ Picnic Sites
- ❑ Restrooms

- ❑ ....
- ❑ ....
- ❑ ....

- ❑ ....
- ❑ ....
- ❑ ....

Rating

⭐ ⭐ ⭐ ⭐ ⭐

Notes

....

....

....

....

....

....

....

....

PASSPORT STAMPS

SCIOTO TRAIL STATE PARK

Ross

DATE(S) VISITED:..

❏ SPRING   ❏ SUMMER   ❏ FALL   ❏ WINTER

WEATHER			TEMP:

❏   ❏   ❏   ❏   ❏   ❏

Address

144 Lake Rd
Chillicothe,
Ohio   45601

About this State Park

A small, quiet park nestled in beautiful 9,000-acre Scioto Trail
State Forest, this state park is an undisturbed wooded refuge
just south of Chillicothe. The ridgetops and winding forest roads
offer breathtaking vistas of the Scioto River Valley. The beauty
and remoteness of Scioto Trail offers the best of escapes to park
visitors.

CHECK IN:

CHECK OUT:

PARK HOURS:

DISTANCE:

FEE(S):..

WILL I RETURN?   ❏ YES   ❏ NO

LODGING:

SIGHTS

WHO I WENT WITH

ACTIVITIES

- ❑ ATV/OHV
- ❑ Berry Picking
- ❑ Biking
- ❑ Boating
- ❑ Canoeing
- ❑ Fishing
- ❑ Hiking
- ❑ Hunting

- ❑ Horseback Riding
- ❑ Kayaking
- ❑ Photography
- ❑ Skiing
- ❑ Skijoring
- ❑ Snowshoeing
- ❑ Snowmobiling
- ❑ Swimming

- ❑ Wildlife
- ❑ Bird Viewing
- ❑ ....
- ❑ ....
- ❑ ....
- ❑ ....
- ❑ ....
- ❑ ....

FACILITIES

- ❑ ADA
- ❑ Gift Shop
- ❑ Museum

- ❑ Visitor Center
- ❑ Picnic Sites
- ❑ Restrooms

- ❑ ....
- ❑ ....
- ❑ ....

- ❑ ....
- ❑ ....
- ❑ ....

Rating

★ ★ ★ ★ ★

Notes

....
....
....
....
....
....
....
....

PASSPORT STAMPS

SHAWNEE STATE PARK

Scioto

DATE(S) VISITED:..

❏ SPRING   ❏ SUMMER   ❏ FALL   ❏ WINTER

WEATHER				TEMP:	
❏	❏	❏	❏	❏	❏

Address

4404 Ohio 125
West Portsmouth,
Ohio 45663

About this State Park

Located in the Appalachian foothills near the banks of the Ohio River, Shawnee State Park is nestled in the 60,000-acre Shawnee State Forest. Once the hunting grounds of the Shawnee Indians, the region is one of the most picturesque in the state, featuring erosion-carved valleys and wooded hills. The rugged beauty of the area has earned it the nickname "The Little Smokies."
Shawnee State Park is open for year-round recreation. There are 15 miles (24 km) of trails open for hiking and some are open to biking. Five pavilions are spread throughout the park along with numerous picnic tables.

CHECK IN:

CHECK OUT:

PARK HOURS:

DISTANCE:

FEE(S):..

WILL I RETURN?   ❏ YES   ❏ NO

LODGING:

WHO I WENT WITH

SIGHTS

ACTIVITIES

❑ ATV/OHV	❑ Horseback Riding	❑ Wildlife
❑ Berry Picking	❑ Kayaking	❑ Bird Viewing
❑ Biking	❑ Photography	❑ ....
❑ Boating	❑ Skiing	❑ ....
❑ Canoeing	❑ Skijoring	❑ ....
❑ Fishing	❑ Snowshoeing	❑ ....
❑ Hiking	❑ Snowmobiling	❑ ....
❑ Hunting	❑ Swimming	❑ ....

FACILITIES

❑ ADA	❑ Visitor Center	❑	❑ ....
❑ Gift Shop	❑ Picnic Sites	❑	❑ ....
❑ Museum	❑ Restrooms	❑	❑ ....

Rating

⭐ ⭐ ⭐ ⭐ ⭐

Notes

....
....
....
....
....
....
....
....

PASSPORT STAMPS

SOUTH BASS ISLAND STATE PARK

Ottawa

DATE(S) VISITED:...

❏ SPRING ❏ SUMMER ❏ FALL ❏ WINTER

WEATHER			TEMP:		
❏	❏	❏	❏	❏	❏

Address

1523 Catawba Ave
Put-In-Bay,
Ohio   43456

About this State Park

The family campground features 125 non-electric sites, and 10 full service sites with electric, water and sewer hook-ups. The campground offers flush toilets, showers, and a dump station. Pet camping is permitted on designated sites. A youth group camp is available by reservation for organized groups. Four cabents, combining the best features of a cabin and tent, are available through a lottery system for weekly rental from Memorial Day to the last weekend in September. A separate lottery is held for rental of the rustic cabin located near the park office.
A picnic shelter, picnic areas, launch ramp, fishing pier and small stone beach area are also available. South Bass Island is accessible by ferry from Port Clinton or Catawba Island.

CHECK IN:

CHECK OUT:

PARK HOURS:

DISTANCE:

FEE(S):...

WILL I RETURN?   ❏ YES   ❏ NO

LODGING:

WHO I WENT WITH

SIGHTS

ACTIVITIES

- ❑ ATV/OHV
- ❑ Berry Picking
- ❑ Biking
- ❑ Boating
- ❑ Canoeing
- ❑ Fishing
- ❑ Hiking
- ❑ Hunting

- ❑ Horseback Riding
- ❑ Kayaking
- ❑ Photography
- ❑ Skiing
- ❑ Skijoring
- ❑ Snowshoeing
- ❑ Snowmobiling
- ❑ Swimming

- ❑ Wildlife
- ❑ Bird Viewing
- ❑ ....
- ❑ ....
- ❑ ....
- ❑ ....
- ❑ ....
- ❑ ....

FACILITIES

- ❑ ADA
- ❑ Gift Shop
- ❑ Museum

- ❑ Visitor Center
- ❑ Picnic Sites
- ❑ Restrooms

- ❑ ....
- ❑ ....
- ❑ ....

- ❑ ....
- ❑ ....
- ❑ ....

Rating

⭐ ⭐ ⭐ ⭐ ⭐

Notes

....
....
....
....
....
....
....
....

PASSPORT STAMPS

SPIEGEL GROVE STATE PARK

Sandusky

DATE(S) VISITED:...

❏ SPRING   ❏ SUMMER   ❏ FALL   ❏ WINTER

| WEATHER | | TEMP: |

❏ ❏ ❏ ❏ ❏ ❏

Address

Fremont, Ohio

About this State Park

Spiegel Grove, also known as Spiegel Grove State Park, Rutherford B. Hayes House, Rutherford B. Hayes Summer Home and Rutherford B. Hayes State Memorial was the estate of Rutherford B. Hayes, the nineteenth President of the United States, located at the corner of Hayes and Buckland Avenues in Fremont, Ohio. Spiegel is the German and Dutch word for mirror. The traditional story is that the estate was named by Hayes' uncle Sardis Birchard, who first built it for his own residence. He named it for the reflective pools of water that collected on the property after a rain shower.

The estate was given to the state for the Spiegel Grove State Park. Since then, the house has been open for tourists as a house museum. For a fee, visitors can view the various rooms as well as furniture, books, and other items in the house. Visitors are allowed to access most of the rooms on the first and second floors. The third and fourth floors are not open to the public.

CHECK IN:

CHECK OUT:

PARK HOURS:

DISTANCE:

FEE(S):..

WILL I RETURN?   ❏ YES   ❏ NO

LODGING:

SIGHTS

WHO I WENT WITH

ACTIVITIES

- ❏ ATV/OHV
- ❏ Berry Picking
- ❏ Biking
- ❏ Boating
- ❏ Canoeing
- ❏ Fishing
- ❏ Hiking
- ❏ Hunting

- ❏ Horseback Riding
- ❏ Kayaking
- ❏ Photography
- ❏ Skiing
- ❏ Skijoring
- ❏ Snowshoeing
- ❏ Snowmobiling
- ❏ Swimming

- ❏ Wildlife
- ❏ Bird Viewing
- ❏ ....
- ❏ ....
- ❏ ....
- ❏ ....
- ❏ ....
- ❏ ....

FACILITIES

- ❏ ADA
- ❏ Gift Shop
- ❏ Museum

- ❏ Visitor Center
- ❏ Picnic Sites
- ❏ Restrooms

- ❏ ....
- ❏ ....
- ❏ ....

- ❏ ....
- ❏ ....
- ❏ ....

Rating

★ ★ ★ ★ ★

Notes

....
....
....
....
....
....
....
....

PASSPORT STAMPS

STONELICK STATE PARK

Clermont

DATE(S) VISITED:...

❑ SPRING   ❑ SUMMER   ❑ FALL   ❑ WINTER

WEATHER		TEMP:			
☀	☀☁	☁	☁☂	☁	☁
❑	❑	❑	❑	❑	❑

Address

2895 Lake Dr
Pleasant Plain,
Ohio   45162-9639

About this State Park

Stonelick State Park is a public recreation area located off Ohio State Route 727, 24 miles (39 km) east of central Cincinnati, in Wayne Township, Clermont County. The state park covers 1,058 acres (428 ha) of land and 200 acres (81 ha) of water. Park activities include fishing, hunting, hiking, picnicking, swimming, boating, and camping.
Stonelick State Park offer a quiet retreat for visitors. The still waters of the lake and stately woodlands provide the setting for a host of outdoor recreational pursuits.

CHECK IN:

CHECK OUT:

PARK HOURS:

DISTANCE:

FEE(S):..

WILL I RETURN?   ❑ YES   ❑ NO

LODGING:

SIGHTS

WHO I WENT WITH

ACTIVITIES

- ❑ ATV/OHV
- ❑ Berry Picking
- ❑ Biking
- ❑ Boating
- ❑ Canoeing
- ❑ Fishing
- ❑ Hiking
- ❑ Hunting

- ❑ Horseback Riding
- ❑ Kayaking
- ❑ Photography
- ❑ Skiing
- ❑ Skijoring
- ❑ Snowshoeing
- ❑ Snowmobiling
- ❑ Swimming

- ❑ Wildlife
- ❑ Bird Viewing
- ❑ ....
- ❑ ....
- ❑ ....
- ❑ ....
- ❑ ....
- ❑ ....

FACILITIES

- ❑ ADA
- ❑ Gift Shop
- ❑ Museum

- ❑ Visitor Center
- ❑ Picnic Sites
- ❑ Restrooms

- ❑ ....
- ❑ ....
- ❑ ....

- ❑ ....
- ❑ ....
- ❑ ....

Rating

★ ★ ★ ★ ★

Notes

....
....
....
....
....
....
....
....

PASSPORT STAMPS

STROUDS RUN STATE PARK

Athens

DATE(S) VISITED:...

❏ SPRING   ❏ SUMMER   ❏ FALL   ❏ WINTER

WEATHER			TEMP:		
☀	✷☁	☁	☁	☁	☁
❏	❏	❏	❏	❏	❏

Address

11661 State Park Rd
Athens, Ohio   45701

About this State Park

Strouds Run State Park is a public recreation area abutting the city of Athens in Athens County. The state park is located primarily in Canaan Township, with a small part in Ames Township. Park boundaries coincide with Athens city limits in several places. The park comprises 2,606 acres (1,055 ha), and includes Dow Lake, a 161-acre (65 ha) artificial lake.
Facilities include a campground (pit toilets, no shower), swimming beach, boat dock, boat and canoe rentals, pistol, picnic grounds and shelters, and hiking trails. Hunting is permitted in season. Shooting ranges are no longer available for the public.
Significant areas of the park are pine plantations (white and red) from the mid-twentieth century, when the land was purchased, originally as the Athens State Forest. There is also one small baldcypress plantation within the park. However, most of the area is mature hardwood forest. The park features many bluffs and rock outcrops of sandstone. Several beaver ponds are within the park boundaries.
Many of the trails are open to mountain bikes.

CHECK IN:

CHECK OUT:

PARK HOURS:

DISTANCE:

FEE(S):...

WILL I RETURN?   ❏ YES   ❏ NO

LODGING:

SIGHTS

WHO I WENT WITH

ACTIVITIES

- ☐ ATV/OHV
- ☐ Berry Picking
- ☐ Biking
- ☐ Boating
- ☐ Canoeing
- ☐ Fishing
- ☐ Hiking
- ☐ Hunting

- ☐ Horseback Riding
- ☐ Kayaking
- ☐ Photography
- ☐ Skiing
- ☐ Skijoring
- ☐ Snowshoeing
- ☐ Snowmobiling
- ☐ Swimming

- ☐ Wildlife
- ☐ Bird Viewing
- ☐ ....
- ☐ ....
- ☐ ....
- ☐ ....
- ☐ ....
- ☐ ....

FACILITIES

- ☐ ADA
- ☐ Gift Shop
- ☐ Museum

- ☐ Visitor Center
- ☐ Picnic Sites
- ☐ Restrooms

- ☐ ....
- ☐ ....
- ☐ ....

- ☐ ....
- ☐ ....
- ☐ ....

Rating

★ ★ ★ ★ ★

Notes

....
....
....
....
....
....
....
....

PASSPORT STAMPS

SYCAMORE STATE PARK

Montgomery

DATE(S) VISITED:..

❑ SPRING   ❑ SUMMER   ❑ FALL   ❑ WINTER

WEATHER	TEMP:
☀ ❄☁ ☁ ☁ ☁ ☁	
❑ ❑ ❑ ❑ ❑ ❑	

Address

4675 Diamond Mill Rd
Dayton, Ohio   45426

About this State Park

Set on 2,384 acres, this park offers a fishing/boating pond,
nature trails, hunting & winter sports.
The meadows, woodlots and still waters of Sycamore State Park
offer an oasis of natural features win the midst of expansive
farmland. Sycamore provides the perfect setting for picnicking,
hiking, fishing and horseback riding.

CHECK IN:

CHECK OUT:

PARK HOURS:

DISTANCE:

FEE(S):..

WILL I RETURN?   ❑ YES   ❑ NO

LODGING:

SIGHTS

WHO I WENT WITH

ACTIVITIES

- ❑ ATV/OHV
- ❑ Berry Picking
- ❑ Biking
- ❑ Boating
- ❑ Canoeing
- ❑ Fishing
- ❑ Hiking
- ❑ Hunting

- ❑ Horseback Riding
- ❑ Kayaking
- ❑ Photography
- ❑ Skiing
- ❑ Skijoring
- ❑ Snowshoeing
- ❑ Snowmobiling
- ❑ Swimming

- ❑ Wildlife
- ❑ Bird Viewing
- ❑ ....
- ❑ ....
- ❑ ....
- ❑ ....
- ❑ ....
- ❑ ....

FACILITIES

- ❑ ADA
- ❑ Gift Shop
- ❑ Museum

- ❑ Visitor Center
- ❑ Picnic Sites
- ❑ Restrooms

- ❑ ....
- ❑ ....
- ❑ ....

- ❑ ....
- ❑ ....
- ❑ ....

Rating

⭐ ⭐ ⭐ ⭐ ⭐

Notes

....
....
....
....
....
....
....
....

PASSPORT STAMPS

TAR HOLLOW STATE PARK

Hocking

DATE(S) VISITED:..

❏ SPRING   ❏ SUMMER   ❏ FALL   ❏ WINTER

Address

16396 Tar Hollow Rd
Laurelville,
Ohio   43135

WEATHER			TEMP:		
❏	❏	❏	❏	❏	❏

About this State Park

Twisting park and forest roads pass through deep ravines and dense woodlands. Scattered shortleaf and pitch pines growing on the ridges were once a source of pine tar for early settlers, hence the name Tar Hollow. Dogwoods, redbuds and a variety of wildflowers color the hillsides in the springtime. Fall's pageant of color is spectacular. Tar Hollow State Park is a public recreation area located five miles south of Laurelville. Surrounded by the foothills of the Appalachian Plateau, the state park is part of a larger protected complex with the adjoining Tar Hollow State Forest. The park offers hiking trails that extend into the state forest in addition to boating, fishing and swimming on 15-acre (6.1 ha) Pine Lake.

CHECK IN:

CHECK OUT:

PARK HOURS:

DISTANCE:

FEE(S):...

WILL I RETURN?   ❏ YES   ❏ NO

LODGING:

SIGHTS

WHO I WENT WITH

ACTIVITIES

❏ ATV/OHV	❏ Horseback Riding	❏ Wildlife
❏ Berry Picking	❏ Kayaking	❏ Bird Viewing
❏ Biking	❏ Photography	❏ ....
❏ Boating	❏ Skiing	❏ ....
❏ Canoeing	❏ Skijoring	❏ ....
❏ Fishing	❏ Snowshoeing	❏ ....
❏ Hiking	❏ Snowmobiling	❏ ....
❏ Hunting	❏ Swimming	❏ ....

FACILITIES

❏ ADA	❏ Visitor Center	❏	❏ ....
❏ Gift Shop	❏ Picnic Sites	❏	❏ ....
❏ Museum	❏ Restrooms	❏	❏ ....

Rating

⭐ ⭐ ⭐ ⭐ ⭐

Notes

....
....
....
....
....
....
....
....

PASSPORT STAMPS

TINKER'S CREEK STATE PARK

Geauga

DATE(S) VISITED:..

❏ SPRING   ❏ SUMMER   ❏ FALL   ❏ WINTER

WEATHER						TEMP:
❏	❏	❏	❏	❏	❏	

Address

10303 Aurora Hudson
Rd, Streetsboro, Ohio
44241

About this State Park

Tinkers Creek State Park is a public recreation area that under the name Tinkers Creek Area is part of Liberty Park in Streetsboro, Portage County. The area's small lakes and marshes provide food and habitat for beavers and thousands of waterfowl. The park offers archery, spring-fed fishing lake, hiking trails, and picnicking areas.

CHECK IN:

CHECK OUT:

PARK HOURS:

DISTANCE:

FEE(S):...

WILL I RETURN?   ❏ YES   ❏ NO

LODGING:

SIGHTS

WHO I WENT WITH

ACTIVITIES

- ❏ ATV/OHV
- ❏ Berry Picking
- ❏ Biking
- ❏ Boating
- ❏ Canoeing
- ❏ Fishing
- ❏ Hiking
- ❏ Hunting

- ❏ Horseback Riding
- ❏ Kayaking
- ❏ Photography
- ❏ Skiing
- ❏ Skijoring
- ❏ Snowshoeing
- ❏ Snowmobiling
- ❏ Swimming

- ❏ Wildlife
- ❏ Bird Viewing
- ❏ ....
- ❏ ....
- ❏ ....
- ❏ ....
- ❏ ....
- ❏ ....

FACILITIES

- ❏ ADA
- ❏ Gift Shop
- ❏ Museum

- ❏ Visitor Center
- ❏ Picnic Sites
- ❏ Restrooms

- ❏ ....
- ❏ ....
- ❏ ....

- ❏ ....
- ❏ ....
- ❏ ....

Rating

★ ★ ★ ★ ★

Notes

....
....
....
....
....
....
....
....

PASSPORT STAMPS

VAN BUREN STATE PARK

Hancock

DATE(S) VISITED:..

❑ SPRING   ❑ SUMMER   ❑ FALL   ❑ WINTER

WEATHER	TEMP:

☀ ❑   ☁ ❑   ☁ ❑   🌧 ❑   ⛈ ❑   🌨 ❑

Address

12259 Township Rd
218 Van Buren,
Ohio   45889

About this State Park

Van Buren State Park is a public recreation area surrounding 45-acre (18 ha) Van Buren Lake in Hancock County. The state park covers 296 acres (120 ha) abutting the southern boundary of the village of Van Buren.
The park features boating for hand- and electric-powered water craft, trails for hikers, mountain bikers and horseback riders, and primitive, full-service and equestrian camping. Fish species found in the lake include largemouth bass, carp, bluegill, channel catfish, bullhead and crappie. Hunting is limited to bowhunting.

CHECK IN:

CHECK OUT:

PARK HOURS:

DISTANCE:

FEE(S):...

WILL I RETURN?   ❑ YES   ❑ NO

LODGING:

SIGHTS

WHO I WENT WITH

ACTIVITIES

❑ ATV/OHV	❑ Horseback Riding	❑ Wildlife
❑ Berry Picking	❑ Kayaking	❑ Bird Viewing
❑ Biking	❑ Photography	❑ ....
❑ Boating	❑ Skiing	❑ ....
❑ Canoeing	❑ Skijoring	❑ ....
❑ Fishing	❑ Snowshoeing	❑ ....
❑ Hiking	❑ Snowmobiling	❑ ....
❑ Hunting	❑ Swimming	❑ ....

FACILITIES

❑ ADA	❑ Visitor Center	❑	❑ ....
❑ Gift Shop	❑ Picnic Sites	❑	❑ ....
❑ Museum	❑ Restrooms	❑	❑ ....

Rating

⭐ ⭐ ⭐ ⭐ ⭐

Notes

....

....

....

....

....

....

....

....

PASSPORT STAMPS

WEST BRANCH STATE PARK

Portage

DATE(S) VISITED:..

❑ SPRING   ❑ SUMMER   ❑ FALL   ❑ WINTER

WEATHER	TEMP:

❑   ❑   ❑   ❑   ❑   ❑

Address

5570 Esworthy Rd
Ravenna, Ohio   44266

About this State Park

West Branch State Park is a public recreation area located east of Ravenna, on the west branch of the Mahoning River. The park encompasses more than 5,000 acres (2,000 ha) of land and 2,650 acres (1,070 ha) of water mainly in Charlestown, Edinburg, and Paris townships, with additional land in neighboring Palmyra, Ravenna, and Rootstown townships. Activities include boating, fishing, and swimming on the Michael J. Kirwan Reservoir, hiking, and camping. The park offers swimming, fishing, camping, boating, 14 miles (23 km) of hiking trails, 20 miles (32 km) of bridle trails, and 12 miles (19 km) of mountain biking trails, winter recreation, and seasonal hunting for deer, small game, and waterfowl.

CHECK IN:

CHECK OUT:

PARK HOURS:

DISTANCE:

FEE(S):..

WILL I RETURN?   ❑ YES   ❑ NO

LODGING:

SIGHTS

WHO I WENT WITH

ACTIVITIES

- ❏ ATV/OHV
- ❏ Berry Picking
- ❏ Biking
- ❏ Boating
- ❏ Canoeing
- ❏ Fishing
- ❏ Hiking
- ❏ Hunting

- ❏ Horseback Riding
- ❏ Kayaking
- ❏ Photography
- ❏ Skiing
- ❏ Skijoring
- ❏ Snowshoeing
- ❏ Snowmobiling
- ❏ Swimming

- ❏ Wildlife
- ❏ Bird Viewing
- ❏ ....
- ❏ ....
- ❏ ....
- ❏ ....
- ❏ ....
- ❏ ....

FACILITIES

- ❏ ADA
- ❏ Gift Shop
- ❏ Museum

- ❏ Visitor Center
- ❏ Picnic Sites
- ❏ Restrooms

- ❏ ....
- ❏ ....
- ❏ ....

- ❏ ....
- ❏ ....
- ❏ ....

Rating

★ ★ ★ ★ ★

Notes

....
....
....
....
....
....
....
....

PASSPORT STAMPS

WOLF RUN STATE PARK

Noble

DATE(S) VISITED:...

❏ SPRING ❏ SUMMER ❏ FALL ❏ WINTER

WEATHER	TEMP:

❏ ❏ ❏ ❏ ❏ ❏

Address

16170 Wolf Run Rd
Caldwell, Ohio   43724

About this State Park

Wolf Run State Park is a 1,338-acre (541 ha) public recreation area located three miles north of the village of Caldwell. The state park features hiking on trails that include a section of the Buckeye Trail plus swimming, boating and fishing on 220-acre (89 ha) Wolf Run Lake.
The rugged hills of southeastern Ohio provide the setting for Wolf Run State Park. The scenic woodlands and cool, clean waters of the park offer visitors a quiet retreat in this remote area of the state.

CHECK IN:

CHECK OUT:

PARK HOURS:

DISTANCE:

FEE(S):..

WILL I RETURN?   ❏ YES   ❏ NO

LODGING:

SIGHTS

WHO I WENT WITH

ACTIVITIES

- ❏ ATV/OHV
- ❏ Berry Picking
- ❏ Biking
- ❏ Boating
- ❏ Canoeing
- ❏ Fishing
- ❏ Hiking
- ❏ Hunting

- ❏ Horseback Riding
- ❏ Kayaking
- ❏ Photography
- ❏ Skiing
- ❏ Skijoring
- ❏ Snowshoeing
- ❏ Snowmobiling
- ❏ Swimming

- ❏ Wildlife
- ❏ Bird Viewing
- ❏ ....
- ❏ ....
- ❏ ....
- ❏ ....
- ❏ ....
- ❏ ....

FACILITIES

- ❏ ADA
- ❏ Gift Shop
- ❏ Museum

- ❏ Visitor Center
- ❏ Picnic Sites
- ❏ Restrooms

- ❏ ....
- ❏ ....
- ❏ ....

- ❏ ....
- ❏ ....
- ❏ ....

Rating

★ ★ ★ ★ ★

Notes

....
....
....
....
....
....
....
....

PASSPORT STAMPS

Made in the USA
Monee, IL
06 July 2022

99181194R00085